EXIT SIGNS

THE EXPRESSWAY TO SELLING
YOUR COMPANY WITH PRIDE AND PROFIT

EXIT SIGNS

PAMELA DENNIS, PhD

SUSTAINABLE BUSINESS PRESS
PORTLAND • OREGON • USA

Published in the United States by Sustainable Business Press
5331 S.W. Macadam Avenue, Suite 258
Portland, Oregon 97239 USA

ISBN: 978-1-942497-07-3
eISBN: 978-1-942497-13-4

Publisher's CIP Data Provided by Quality Books, Inc.

Dennis, Pamela.
Exit signs: the expressway to selling your company
with pride and profit / Pamela Dennis, PhD
pages cm
Includes bibliographical references and index.
LCCN 2015942229
ISBN 978-1-942497-07-3
eISBN 978-1-942497-13-4
1. Sale of business enterprises.   I. Title.
HD1393.25.D46 2015   658.1'64
QBI15-600137

Printed simultaneously in the United States of America
the United Kingdom and Australia

3 5 7 9 10 8 6 4

TABLE OF CONTENTS

ACKNOWLEDGMENTS

No one works harder than business owners, whether they own a small medical practice or a 400 person manufacturing firm with overseas operations. They impact trillions of dollars of assets in our country. I celebrate their passion, dedication and contribution to local economies and communities. There are a special thirty or so who agreed to be interviewed with the promise of anonymity. I owe them a special thanks for sharing their stories about starting, building, and leaving their 'babies.' In some cases they were in the midst of trying to figure out how to exit, and they candidly shared their challenges.

I am grateful to my team who helped me on my journey of writing and publishing. It was a long trip. I was a driver who resisted every social media task from web sites to blogs to Twitter accounts. Sometimes they had to take over the wheel to keep me moving forward. Tea Silvestre of Story Bistro, thanks for teaching me so much I never thought I wanted to know about social media and building a strong platform. Max Regan, writing coach, I will miss our usual table at the Tea House. Lisbeth Tanz, of the Hired Pen, you are amazing at the detail of editing and helping me learn at last where the comma goes. Susanna Donato saved me from drowning in the details and reminding me when I forgot a few. Lieve Maas of Bright Light Graphics, was so patient and brilliant at translating my vision for the look and feel of the book. Denise Williams at Six Degrees Publishing Group spent hours sharing her expertise about publishing; kept me out of trouble, and pulled all of the pieces together. If I only knew then what I know now…

It's funny; I started my own company thinking I would have more discretionary time. Ha! Every owner knows that's unrealistic. I sold my business to have more discretionary time. Ha! Most Boomer retirees say they are so busy they don't know how they ever had time to work. I began this book thinking it would be a contemplative part of my precious discretionary time. Double Ha! So I got a little cranky at times. Thanks to friends and family I didn't park in that mental state. Thank you to Jim, my stealth supporter (despite asking too many times, "Are you ever going to finish?"). Thank you to Morgan, Brenda, Andy, Jane, Mike and Marilyn, Priscilla, Fran, Meg, Laurie, Ron, Amy, John and Gail, Sue and Barry, and all the rest of my buddies. They say you should never drink and drive. Thank goodness you all shared a drink and a laugh now and then along this writing journey. You kept me moving forward. Cheers.

INTRODUCTION ~ FINDING YOUR ROADMAP

All changes, even the most longed for have their melancholy; for what we leave behind is a part of ourselves.

Anatole France

A Map for the Journey Ahead

On a scale of one to ten, what is your level of dread versus excitement at the thought of selling and leaving your business? Do you relish and anticipate the imagined freedom of exploring a new phase of life? Or, does leaving create anxiety, maybe even a gut-wrenching fear of irrelevance and loss of identity? Chances are you probably bounce around the continuum depending on the day. What you need, more than anything, is a plan designed to realize your hopes and eliminate your anxiety and dread. Yet 87 percent of small business owners don't have an exit plan, and it will cost them dearly.[1]

* * *

Before there were Google Maps, GPS, and onboard navigation systems, when our family took a vacation, Mom would go to the AAA Auto Club office for a TripTik™. This indispensable tool was a simple spiral bound pamphlet of carefully selected maps highlighting the route we would take and where we might stay or stop to sightsee. As we drove, those customized maps were our lifeline. We knew we could make choices along the way, but that little packet gave us confidence for the trip ahead.

As a business owner, you are also choosing destinations whether you call them dreams, visions or business plans. If only every business came with a packet of roadmaps as compact, neat and unambiguous as a TripTik.

Selling a business also means you need to know your destination and have a custom-built roadmap that leads you out of a business to which you have so passionately committed the greatest part of your life. That map must deliver you to a destination characterized by three things: a profitable sale, pride in leaving a strong, sustainable business, and serenity in knowing you have a legacy and a path forward.

Putting together a useful set of maps for an exit journey is the ultimate internal conflict. You want the freedom from obligations but the security and sense of purpose your business provides. You wonder, "Why bother to plan?" when even the best of them, whether a yearly operating plan or a five-year strategy, are turned upside down by unexpected events – economic, market and technology fluctuations, loss of key talent or customers and even team dynamics. But those owners who overcome the dread or skepticism and create exit plans report less stress and anxiety as their exit approaches. In fact those who successfully sell their companies overwhelmingly wish they had begun planning earlier.

This book gives you the information to plan your exit journey. It helps you make decisions about how to leave your business with pride and control, even in the midst of unpredictable conditions. My goal is to provide you with the tools you need to simplify preparing both yourself and your organization for the transitions involved in exiting your business with pride and profit.

Gathering Information and Insight

Information is vital; but in preparing to sell your business, it isn't enough. You also need insight about your habits, thinking and motivations. When you have insight into those things, you can act with more speed and wisdom on the information involved in selling and leaving your business.

Information plus insight will help you:

- Assess your intentions and aspirations for life beyond your company
- Evaluate the readiness and health of your company (and your personal leadership behavior) for a successful transition
- Develop a plan to exit your business profitably, confident that it will continue with its mission, reputation, culture and operations.
- Carry out your exit strategy and transition plans with commitment and discipline

Perhaps your comfort zone as a business owner is your technical expertise: in marketing, technology, finance, or a specific industry. Preparing your company for your departure is a different kind of work. It takes organizational change and leadership skill to step back from the distinct, daily, and familiar work of running your business, to planning for an ambiguous and evolving future and leading the transitions involved in the transfer of ownership.

This leadership work means focusing on all that can be messy, irrational, conflict-ridden and "soft." This work is inescapable no matter how much we wish to avoid it. It tests our tolerance for ambiguity about our future; for planning and process and, for the stress that we feel devoting energy and precious time to topics other than the "real work" of financials, a product launch or sales.

It takes courage to start this work and commitment to finish it. *Exit Signs* shows you the way to be known for both of these leadership characteristics.

Owners Shifting Gears

There are 22.7 million small to medium sized (SME) businesses in the US. They produce 47 percent of the non-farm GDP and employ over 48 percent of private sector payrolls (as of 2011).[2] The asset value of these businesses is estimated at over $10 trillion. Among that group of asset owners are twelve million Boomer business owners who are hoping to transfer ownership in the next five to ten years. Behind them are the Gen X business owners looking ahead ten-plus years to the sale of their businesses.

These owners are counting on the sale of their business to fund retirement or encore careers, but the liquidation of these companies affects more than individuals. The ripple effect of the ownership transfer will also impact communities and the national economy as, unfortunately, only one in three or four businesses cash out as desired, and almost 20 percent simply close their doors.[3] This trend has held steady for decades. Research says lack of planning is the major reason for these dismal results.[4]

If you are like many late-stage business owners, you have an aggressive timeline for exiting your businesses, especially if you feel you've had to delay your exit due to the financial crash of 2008. If you are a forward-thinking, mid-stage business owner you have a bit more to plan your exit. In either case consider these buyer groups:

- Some Boomer are buyers, looking for their Fourth Quarter career move from corporate life to small business owner – think "Late Bloomers"
- Gen X Buyers are ready to take over the reins of a business versus creating a start-up – think "Ready to Wear"
- Cash-rich companies are looking to vertically integrate or take out a competitor while prices are low.

Anyone in these buyer pools may be interested in purchasing your company – but only when they see great value. *Exit Signs* helps prepare you and your company for the sales process and the transition of ownership.

The mainstream books and blogs written to help owners sell their business are, in general, for two groups: the "build-to-flip" entrepreneurs and for distressed owners with flat or declining growth who need to sell their business to another company, cash out quickly or get growth capital via a private equity group.

But there is an important third group, that wave of sellers who founded and worked tirelessly to build an enduring entity. They want to see their brainchild ("my baby"), often their life's work, sustained when their tenure at the helm is over. It is for these business owners that this book is written.

The 22.7 million small to medium sized enterprise owners who will eventually step away from their businesses need a roadmap that recognizes their long history of vision, passion, and dedication to making their business successful, and the natural exhaustion that accompanies years of growing and running a business. Generations today who consider end-career and retirement concepts to be theirs to redefine need a new kind of roadmap for their exit journey that recognizes their aspirations and values of built to last versus built to flip companies. Unfortunately, while 96 percent of business owners agree they need an exit plan, only 13 percent have a written plan.[5]

Your Goal, Route and Directions

At the end of a long journey, there is nothing better than to feel gratified and fulfilled by what you have accomplished. This feeling is true whether it is an endurance bicycle race, a cross-country vacation or turning over the keys to a business. Coupled with that good feeling is the desire to be rewarded for the planning, commitment and investment you have made that provides for your (or others') future. You feel you've earned a healthy return on investment. In *Exit Signs,* there is a third important goal: that what you have created lives on after you leave. Call it a legacy or sustainability; it is also necessary to your definition of success.

This book describes three legs to your journey, three milestones that ensure you have: a strategy you can execute, company plans for a sustainable future, and a sense of serenity that you have done it well, have closure, and see a path forward. These three legs contain ten directions for exiting your business with pride, profit and a legacy.

The route follows a timeline of 24 to 30 months, the typical time required to execute an exit plan and sell a business. Your journey's legs are:

From Aspiration to Exit Strategy

Three of our ten route directions address your desired end-state – for the business and you. This includes understanding your personal motivations and aspirations, exit timing and hopes for your company after you sell. These directions also lead you through a reality check on the state of your business health and of your leadership that impact a successful transition. Finally, as you exit this leg of the journey you have a list of prioritized improvements that will tune up your business and prepare for a salable company.

Sustainable and Ready for Sale

Four of the ten directions address sustainability and the value-producing activities such as succession planning, process reliability, communication, customer retention and revenue sustainability.

Letting Go with Serenity

Finally, three steps guide you through the process of letting go with serenity. They help you achieve three things: closure on the preparation for your exit; confidence your people in good hands; and some composure about what lies ahead for you. You are prepared to let go and move on. Your last step captures the learning from the experience.

Each of these ten directions tells you what to focus on, what *questions* to answer and some of the information you need for decision-making. And along your journey *you need a rest stop*. That's why there are Scenic Overlooks, places where you stop, reflect and apply what you have just read to make it practical and provide you with deeper insight. They support you to examine your company, your people and prospective buyers to see what you might do to accelerate achieving your goals.

This book helps you tap into the skills and motivation and experience used to *run* your business year after year and apply that same motivation to learning how to *leave* your business.

Your Navigator

In case it isn't obvious, I am of the Boomer generation. I also built and sold a successful small business. I spent thirty years as an internal and external organization and leadership development consultant including twenty as a business owner.

In my technical role as an organization development consultant, I worked with organizations from *Fortune* 100 to *Inc.* 500 firms to emerging companies and small partnerships on leading change, productivity improvement and executive leadership. I advised CEOs and future CEOs through growth periods and tough times. Like all those who love their fields and value making a difference, the work was incredibly rewarding.

In my business-owner role, I wore many hats: business development, account executive to major international clients, CFO and signatory on leases and lines of credit, and partner/team member. This too was gratifying both financially and emotionally as we built a unique community of clients and colleagues.

When I sold my firm, we held a Farewell Pamela party that was a great illustration of who we became as a company. I looked out into the audience of 60 or so people and saw clients, friends and colleagues (a lovely redundancy) from Australia, Europe, South America, Canada and all across the US; partners from our offices in Melbourne, Boulder, and Palo Alto. We had grown beyond our wildest dreams and thrived as a broad community.

Saying farewell, I felt proud and optimistic. We were sustainable with long-term contracts in place and excellent cash flow. We had new promising partners. We had no debt but way too many frequent flier miles. I had a profitable payout. These results were possible because we had stepped back from the day-to-day to put in place a four-year roadmap for the phased transition of ownership.

Was there melancholy that lovely winter evening? Yes, but there was also serenity in the accomplishment, financial reward and the deep connection to those who had shared the journey and were prepared to continue it. In stepping away, you are leaving *behind* a part of you, but you also leave with a treasure of experiences, relationships and learning. This book is, in part, a way to convey the lessons of that journey – lessons from leading and owning a business and from working with business owners and leaders. I hope it conveys the importance of leading in ways that let you leave your business profitably, with pride in building its sustainability, and with a sense of serenity that you made a difference and have a path forward.

Are you ready? Then let's roll down the windows, turn up the stereo and hit the road!

FIRST LEG

FROM ASPIRATION TO STRATEGY

Directions

STEP 1. COMMIT TO THE TRIP

Generational Perspectives Matter

Clarify the Legacy You Want to Leave

Recognize Your Road Hazards and Find Alternate Routes

SCENIC OVERLOOK: BUILDING INSIGHT AND FINDING MEANING

STEP 2. MAP YOUR DESTINATION

Declare Your Personal Goals, Business Objectives and Timing

Select Your Pit Crew of Technical Advisors

Find Your Motivation: Why Go Through the Pain?

SCENIC OVERLOOK: SETTING THE COURSE

STEP 3. CHECK YOUR DASHBOARD INDICATORS

Set Your Organizational Health Gauges

Conduct a Dashboard Reality Check

Set Your Priority Transition Plans

SCENIC OVERLOOK: CHECKING REALITY TOOLS

STEP 1 ~ COMMIT TO THE TRIP

Never Trust Anyone Over 30.

Abbie Hoffman

You have three requirements for your exit destination. That it produces: 1) a healthy profit, 2) pride in leaving a sustainable company for your people and the new owner and 3) a feeling of serenity with your legacy and your path forward. Step 1, Commit to the Trip, prepares you for the level of commitment required to accomplish those outcomes.

GENERATIONAL PERSPECTIVES MATTER

As the Baby Boomer population bulge (born 1946 to 1964) descends on our economy, to be overtaken by the Gen X-ers by the late 2020s, the business owners of these generations will have a prolonged disruptive impact on the transfer of businesses.

First, about half of the U.S. job base will face a transition where historically only one in three or four businesses are successful in transferring. Second, let's say each business is worth an average of a million dollars. If only one in four businesses sells, the U.S. could lose $30 trillion in economic wealth.[6]

For the sake of millions of employees and their communities, business owners need to improve the odds of a successful sale of a sustainable business. It begins with owners' perspectives about their businesses – and about leaving them.

Redefining Retirement

"Baby Boomers fundamentally will reinvent retirement" says the conclusion to a major retirement survey.[7] Boomers are merely pioneering the redefinition. Multiple reports on retirement trends found that, unlike our parents or grandparents who looked forward to the golden years of retirement, Boomers and the first 401k generation, Gen X, both envision a phased retirement and a very full life in their next phase[8]. Sixty-five percent of Baby Boomer workers plan to work past age 65 or do not plan to retire. Among Generation X, 54 percent also plan to retire later than 65 or do not plan to retire.[9]

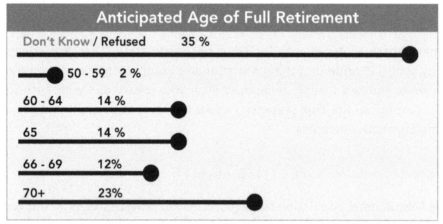

Anticipated Age of Full Retirement

Don't Know / Refused	35 %
50 - 59	2 %
60 - 64	14 %
65	14 %
66 - 69	12%
70+	23%

Survey populations Americans currently age 50-66 and not yet retired, 2002.
Source: *Insured Retirement Institute*

A friend recently asked her 65-year-old husband who owned a successful medical practice if he planned to work until he was 80. He paused for quite a while and said, "I don't know." Because he couldn't imagine what he would do if he didn't go to his office, he couldn't think about a plan to leave it. He is in good company; 35 percent answered "don't know" to the "when?" question.

Today's mid- and late-career business owners don't see retirement and selling their business as pulling off the road and permanently parking the car. A number of book titles capture this vision. *Retire Retirement, Generation Ageless* and *Don't Retire, Rewire* all suggest that regardless of generation *we all* want to define and control our destiny.

It is estimated that 31 million Americans age 44 to 70 are interested in "encore careers," namely, "pursuits that enable individual to put their passion to work for the greater good."[10] When asked about their ideal retirement work arrangement, the most common choices were to:

- Repeatedly "cycle" between periods of work and leisure (42%)
- Have part-time work (16%)
- Start a business (13%)
- Work full time (6%)

"Baby Boomer women are dreaming of retiring to Mars while Baby Boomer men hope to retire to Venus[11]*. "*

Generational retirement views are a study in diversity in another way – gender differences. Baby Boomer men are looking forward to working less, relaxing more and spending more time with their spouse. Baby Boomer women see the dual liberations of empty nests and retirement as an opportunity for career development, community involvement and continued personal growth.[12] It reminds me of a friend whose CEO husband retired and then asked her one day shortly afterward, "Honey what's for lunch?" This active community volunteer during her "career days" said calmly, "I didn't make your lunch before you retired, I don't make your lunch now that you are."

For business couples, selling the company and retiring can be stressful on their relationship, and 1.2 million husband/wife company owners are going to have to figure out how lunch is provided. They will also have to decide what their retirement destination looks like when they exit their businesses. Only 39 percent of married couples, in general, say they and their spouse share a similar vision for retirement.[13] It is no wonder that the fastest growing divorce rate is within the over 50-age group.[14]

Most people would not unilaterally decide to sell their home, stage it and list it without a thorough discussion of the question of, "Then what?" unless it was a novel divorce strategy. According to a recent annual survey of 5,400 U.S. households, many couples do the equivalent when they look at retirement. Only 38 percent of couples engage in retirement planning together.[15] One CEO I interviewed related his approach to working through this important decision by saying, "I told my board my plan and then went home and told my wife who said, 'Oh really?'"

Wise business-owner couples know change presents challenges and opportunities that require dedicated attention. These couples have serious planning work to do together. They must consider what the common vision is, who is ready and who is not, what the financial goals are, what the timing is and, importantly, what the profile of the next owner needs to be. They must also consider how their relationship could evolve into the next phase of life together. The Scenic Overlook work at the end of this chapter will help begin that discussion.

Self-Image and World View of Four Generations

Every generation believes it is unique. The Pew Research Center asked individuals in four population groups "What makes your generation unique?" The table below summarizes the key descriptors for each group.[16] Here is how self-image may affect the buyer-seller interactions and the perceived value of a business to different generations.

MILLENIALS	GEN X	BOOMERS	TRADITIONALISTS
1981-1997	1965-1980	1946-1964	1928-1945
Technology use 24%	Technology use 12%	Work ethic 17%	WWII, Depression 14%
Music/Pop culture 11%	Work Ethic 11%	Respectful 14%	Smarter 13%
Liberal/Tolerant 7%	Conservative/Trad'l 7%	Values/Morals 8%	Honest 12%
Smarter 6%	Smarter 6%	"Baby Boomers" 6%	Values/Morals 10%
Clothes 5%	Respectful 5%	Smarter 5%	Work Ethic 10%

How Generations Describe their Uniqueness

Note: *Top five responses for each group based on open-ended questions vs. list of options.*
Source: *Pew Research Center, "Millennials: Confident, Connected, Open to Change," February 2010.*
Generation Category Dates: *Pew Research Center Fact Tank, January 2015.*

a. Regardless of generation, one self-concept holds constant: we all think we are smarter than other generations. So be smart, but also be WISE! You know what brings value in your business; make it clear with complete, well-analyzed information in your company story. Be wise by using the same great skills with buyers that you use with your customers. Show respect for a buyer's experience and knowledge regardless of age or generation. Think of harmonies, not comparison.

In multi-generation family businesses, show you value the perspective and education of the next generation by inviting them to strategy or other business discussions. Let them hear how you think and allow them to offer their views. Intergenerational conflicts and family dynamics are aggravated over perceptions of who is *smarter,* the *right way to* ... and even over what *experience* counts and who should be teaching whom.

Conversations, information sharing and negotiations based on mutual respect for intelligence, even when there are significance differences in experience or backgrounds, is critical. The sustainability of the company will depend on other smart people who see new possibilities.

b. Millennials do not list "work ethic" as a distinction of their group. Rethink your interpretation of "work ethic." Millennials' work habits are fueled by work *in service to* a higher purpose. Describe how your company and its products, services and key relationships provide a benefit beyond profit. What mark has your company left on the community, your people or maybe the advancement of an industry or body of knowledge? These things will get Millennials' attention. By finding the mutual interest in a higher purpose, you will bridge the perception of an important generation gap. The members of a younger generation cannot hear the *"what you have to sell"* before they understand the *"why you exist."*

c. Technology is the great divide between pre- and post-1965. Assess the ability of your business to compete successfully beyond your leadership. Are the systems and technology all in your head? Do your current systems and technologies help you reach your markets and customers? Is your business compliant in the most cost-effective ways, or are you relying on "how we have always done it?"

The lack of tech tools can reduce the value of a company (from systems to web-based marketing) and salability. When younger generation buyers see additional investment is needed to bring the business into the 21st century, they will likely have two responses. They will either reduce the offer price, or wonder what else in the business is out of date believing they are, in fact, smarter than you and more open to change.

In order for GenX or Millennials to be your successor, they will need hands-on, fast-paced learning opportunities and engage in technology applications/efficiencies. Their engagement level is different from Boomers' whose attention to tending long-established relationships and sharing stories are most valued and seen as teaching tools. However, while relationships and stories are important, they won't have the same appeal or draw for younger generations.

Here's a case in point. A relatively new business owner, a GenX grandson, acquired the family inn business in a *generation skipping* transfer. His Boomer parents were not interested in ownership and its implications. His Traditionalist grandparents had developed a well-run, beautiful inn with excellent, efficient operations and a reputation for wonderful personalized service.

The industry was changing and demanding more internet marketing, web-based strategies and online tools. The founding generation did not have the skills or the interest in learning these new ways of doing business. The grandson, who was in search of his passion and a place to raise his family, was offered the business. It was a terrific match. He had a desire to learn and carry on the business built on fond memories of working summers at the inn. He recognized the value built around operational efficiencies and staff training that his grandparents had established in the business, and he was excited about the technology challenge.

Another generational distinction is important in selling your business. There is a growing trend among retiring Boomers to think about buying and running an existing business. The pool of potential buyers for your business will also include Boomers. These prospective buyers have the leadership experience, a healthy balance sheet and are unlike many in the younger generations who have become more financially risk-averse because of the Great Recession.

Successful business owners have the smarts, values, and action orientation to use generational differences to achieve their exit goals, but we don't always utilize them. A study by Fidelity Investments found that more than half of retirees looked back on their years before retirement and wished they had done more to prepare.[17] Lack of insight into our unique perspective along with procrastination guarantees owners will end up on a road with an exit sign labeled *disappointment*.

CLARIFY THE LEGACY YOU WANT TO LEAVE

Are we being good ancestors?

Jonas Salk

We think of a legacy as what iconic figures leave behind for the rest of us to admire or aspire to like the legacies of Jackie Robinson, Mother Teresa, Steve Jobs, The Dali Lama, Albert Einstein, Helen Keller.

Your legacy begins with your intentions and aspirations. Jiminy Cricket told us wisely, "If you don't have a dream, how can you make a dream come true?" Your aspiration could involve many things: your company's reputation, financial security for your people or family, leaving a new body of knowledge or a lasting effect in your community.

Your vision for your business might be your desired legacy, or it may be the answer to the broader question of "How do I measure my life?" Surveys show that companies with a clear, higher purpose are more profitable and have higher employee and customer loyalty. Further, leaders who have their sights on a future horizon are among the most admired.[18]

You may be thinking that legacy, vision and aspiration sound like *pie in the sky* notions. They can be unless they are used to shape your company culture, strategy and operating systems, the things that grow your business and make it a great place to work. Then *pie in the sky* becomes *rubber on the road* to making a legacy achievable.

Below are two examples of how legacy, vision and aspirations can fuel a business.

Not many founders so intentionally imagine their companies when they take the helm as Thomas Watson, Sr. did when he took over The Computing, Tabulating and Recording Co. You know it today as IBM. His vision fueled IBM's ability to shape a legacy. He described three reasons behind IBM becoming what it did.

The first reason he gave was he had a "very clear picture of what the company would look like when it was finally done", i.e., his vision was clear to him. His second reason was that he translated his dream into actions and practices that people could see. And the third reason was to begin acting that way from the beginning. "In other words, I realized that for IBM to become a great company it would have to act like a great company long before it ever became one.[19]

The second example, while less famous, is a bit more concrete.

When I wrote my two-page business plan for a consulting business, I declared what I valued and for what I wanted to be known. These were my early aspirations:

- Positively affect how it felt to work in an organization in ways that improved the bottom-line
- Build a business that would endure beyond me and where everyone would share in the benefits
- Be "outrageously successful" in terms of real profits and increasing equity
- Compete with the big name consulting firms for the big jobs, yet be known for never acting like a big name consulting firm

These aspirations had impact only when we translated them into our company practices, strategies, operating plans, measures and budgets.

Think About the End Game Now

Without aspiration, planning has no answer to the question of "to what end?" Without plans, aspiration lacks a tether to action. If you want to leave a legacy, you must declare your intention or purpose and then translate it into strategy, culture and explicit operating plans. Whether you did this upon forming your company or as you think about selling it, making it explicit is your leadership task.

The same is true in beginning the exit process. You must declare your desired end game if you plan to achieve it. However, according to the Small Business Administration (SBA), most business owners who begin the exit process usually fail because they failed to plan. In fact, the overwhelming majority of those who do plan feel as if they began the process late.[20]

A CEO working through his exit plan provided a good example of clarity. "My goal for my remaining tenure is to leave my company iron-clad viable with leaders who believe in it and can pick it up – even though I could get more money selling it to a third party."

As you move down the road to realizing your legacy at your exit, it can feel a bit like driving the freeways of Southern California. You sure better know where you are headed each time you enter those six lanes (in each direction) and massive traffic – all going 80 miles per hour in a 65-mile-per-hour speed zone. You don't want to be caught in the far-left lane when you need to exit quickly on the right. On the road and in selling your business, you must know your destination, how to navigate the route and be aware of the exit signs along the way.

Fortunately, most of the time, you lead your company in the right-hand lanes. By doing this, you react to the ebb and flow of events day-to-day, make lane changes and avoid road hazards, such as customer and people issues and market shifts. However, these same lanes are what give us tight shoulders and headaches if we never get out of them.

Sometimes, you take the dedicated High Occupancy Vehicle (HOV) or express lane, which accelerates progress. Your *company* HOV lane makes you step back and ask, "What is our long-term strategy?" or "How do we continue to engage and grow our people?" You can't spend all your time in that lane, though, because there are no direct exits off an HOV to your actual destination.

Realizing our legacy is never a single lane or a straight line. It requires patience, dedication, agility and giving up the delusion that you can control traffic! Thinking about your legacy allows you to move beyond short-term definitions of success. The best leaders learn to hold on to a sense of larger purpose while also leading the day-to-day demands of executing on yearly goals and operating plans. Those who don't may be the basis for Mr. Spock's comment, *"Curious how often you humans manage to obtain that which you do not want."*[21]

ASK YOURSELF

What is the legacy I hope to have created when I leave my company?
- What is in place already?
- What remains to be done?

RECOGNIZE YOUR ROAD HAZARDS AND FIND ALTERNATE ROUTES

We all dislike road hazards that can delay, cause an accident or create a detour. They exist, too, in your business, but business hazards usually lack effective signage. Like a good driver, you look ahead to find early warning signs and alternate routes. Many hazards have uncontrollable external causes, such as a major recession or the death of a partner. These events create anxiety, but they also generate energy to find a way through or around them. Becoming inventive and determined when hazards appear is paramount.

Sometimes though, road hazards are hidden. These require a different kind of attentiveness. These hazards lie *within you,* keeping you from seeing how to take the time to plan your exit. As Pogo observed, sometimes "We have met the enemy and he is us."

Three types of hazards explain why many company sales are often poorly executed. These are:

- "Too Busy to Leave, Too Tired to Stay"
- "A Bigger Engine – The Money Seduction"
- "Making the Tough Calls"

Road Hazard: Too Busy to Leave, Too Tired to Stay.

Do you ever feel like that? You are so busy running your business you don't have the time to think about how to leave it. You may be so busy and exhausted by the daily demands over many years that while leaving is on your mind, taking the time for exit planning gets pushed to the back burner.

It's no wonder. You are the fuel of ideas, the engine that powers your company forward, the shocks that provide stability and a smooth ride. You are so busy performing all those functions, some of which you may detest, that it's an effort just moving down the road directly in front of you. Never mind looking out two years to accomplish an exit plan.

Some call working too much "workaholism." The important difference between being too busy and being a workaholic is being *pulled to work* because it brings us satisfaction and enjoyment and *pushed to work* because of an obsession. The research shows that it isn't how hard you work, but why and how you work hard that determines the effect work has on your health and your social environment.[22] For most business owners, the *pull* keeps us grounded and passionate.

Here are some warning signs of this road hazard. Which of these are true of you?

- Do you believe only your hands-on management and attention will bring the control or performance you desire?
- When you take a vacation, are you tied to your emails and mobile phone? Are you uncomfortable sitting quietly for 20 to 30 minutes and being "in the moment"?

- Do you equate being busy with being productive and effective? E.g., at home, are you reviewing reports on your stationary bike, that is, when you don't skip the workout?
- Do you see yourself primarily as The Business Owner vs. also having an important role of parent, spouse, friend, son or daughter?

If you answered many of these questions "yes", you face a powerful road hazard to achieving your exit strategy. You are not alone, as many business owners who do not have an exit strategy face it, too. Seeing the hazard is the first step. Building alternate routes follows this insight.

Alternate Routes — Rerouting Your Self-Discipline

Every day we make choices about our activities, attitude and priorities. If our goal is to exit the business profitably and with a legacy, how do we keep that foremost in our mind so that it is the basis for different choices about our time, attention and relationships? How do we self-advocate making the changes we know we need? Here are three suggested alternate routes.

Route 1 - Define Your WHY: Studies tells us that those who have higher work enjoyment, less stress and more energy tend to work for a higher purpose. Purpose, not perfection, releases the fuel for exit planning.

A colleague had a successful corporate education company. He was a Big Thinker and liked to generate Big Ideas that made Big Change happen. He wanted to get off the corporate treadmill, but he loved what he did. So he set up a non-profit to bring the benefits of his corporate work into public schools. Of course, that meant twice the mental work and pressure to create Big Results. It wasn't until he looked at his habit of going *Big* that he could change this success measure to Engage My Heart. He picked a single college class to mentor each semester supported by a great workbook he created. This new purpose dramatically changed his energy, focus and ability to sell his company.

ASK YOURSELF

How can you bring a higher purpose into your work, or your life outside of work, to renew your focus and find the energy to plan your exit?

Route 2 - Self-Talk: Did you know that the very act of setting a goal fosters its achievement? When you write down your exit goals, you mentally begin working toward them. You create a voice of the future to counter the voice of the status quo. When you can see the gap between where you are versus your goal, you have a greater likelihood of reaching it.

ASK YOURSELF

What are your goals and dreams for a successful exit from your business? What is the gap between how things are and how you would like them to be?

Finally, did you know that the more you believe *you* are in control of your destiny, the more you tend to find ways to make a change happen? For a change to happen, you have to make it clear to yourself who is in charge of closing the gap – you or the old habit.

ASK YOURSELF

Who is going to make the decision each time your anxiety escalates about "if I don't handle this now" or "if I don't do this myself?" Will it be the old *Too Busy* control person or you, who wants to celebrate the sale of a healthy business and enjoy the next phase of life?

Route 3 - Share: Redirecting your self-discipline also requires others' support, so tell others what you are trying to change and how they can help you. Friends and colleagues are vital to eliminating a road hazard. That's why efforts like diet centers, AA, and social media sites, create and uses affinity groups. Such groups work because they know your goal and its importance to you. They hear your progress and celebrate your milestones, and help you when you backslide. Here is a simple example.

When I left my company, I made a bet with a friend that I would not transfer my crazed business owner and consulting life to a pile of independent consulting. The prize was a case of pricey wine. I wagered that any consulting work would not exceed 30 days in my first post-departure year. I faithfully reported quarterly over lunch. My friend served as my conscience. The bet provided just the right amount of competitive spirit I needed from a friend. In the end, I won the bet. I sometimes wonder if I would have been so disciplined and aware of my time if I hadn't made that bet and had his support.

 ASK YOURSELF

What does social support look like for you as an alternate route to *Too Busy – Too Tired?* Whom might you let in on your challenge, your goal and your progress?

Road Hazard: A Bigger Engine

Nothing hooks us like size be it an engine, a boat, diamond, or serving of great fries – "Supersize me!" If you type "grow your business" into a search engine, you will get 53 million results.

A hazard in your exit path is the opportunity to stay *one more year* to accomplish one last growth challenge. It appeals to our ego of being needed, and it validates our experience and record of accomplishment. The next story will help you think about how to respond to this "Bigger Engine" hazard. It has three parts: the hook, the hazard and hindsight lessons.

Our firm had a track record of consistent growth: 15 to 20 percent per year for almost 20 years. Some years the growth was 50 percent. Profit and partners' personal incomes nicely tracked revenues. Twelve months before my exit date, the major tasks in our continuity plans had been completed. The new equity partners had come on board or been promoted, and we were about to open an Australian office with a new Aussie partner. Then the potential for 50 percent new growth over the next two years made us question the timing of my departure.

The Hook: We could make our "$5 million by '05" goal early. We could transfer the relationship of our biggest client to a key partner. I could keep doing what I loved best – lead big projects and develop new business opportunities. Lastly, my buyout would be more secure.

The Hazard: If I stayed, would it lessen the pressure on other partners to step into the role of rainmakers? How would extending buyout obligations affect profits and bonuses given our employment and exit agreements? Having been in what seemed like a Daytona 500 race for 18 years, how would adding "one more lap" on a near empty gas tank affect me and my home life?

We decided I would stay another year focusing on major contract negotiations and succession. In addition, I would be mentoring our new Aussie partner, opening the Melbourne office and transferring my relationship with our largest client to my Second Lieutenant.

The Hindsight: We doubled our revenues and exceeded the 2005 growth target by a million dollars two years early. We won a two-year multi-million dollar contract extension, and the CEO of our largest client sent a personal thank you for the great new account leader. The Lord Mayor of Melbourne officially welcomed us during our office grand opening. While our international growth captured our attention, we lost our U.S. business focus. That busy final year added to my exhaustion and sense of burnout. In hindsight, I wondered if we had considered all the possible options.

ASK YOURSELF

The questions you must answer when extending your exit date are:

Would a delayed exit:
- make your business stronger, positively impact customers and influence key talent development and retention, especially identified successors?
- risk that a change in market conditions or the pool of potential buyers would adversely impact your goals?

What other options are there to achieve your objective or opportunity?
- what would support those options?
- what would these options permit that a delay or not?

How would staying on longer affect
- you and your family?
- your exit strategy?

Alternate Routes

The alternate routes below suggest you step back before deciding to extend your departure date and get additional perspectives on the cost-benefits. Look at all of your business objectives, not just growth. Search for multiple options or approaches.

Route 1 - Take a Coffee Break: One alternate route is to take a break from driving to hold robust discussions with your team and external advisors about the many factors involved in the decision to delay your exit. Answer the questions posed above. Hold the same candid discussion with the significant others in your life for another perspective on the larger question of "What about this change works for your/our life?"

Route 2 - Take a Family Detour: If you are the head of a family-owned business, it is particularly hard *not* to take an extra lap, especially if heirs are not ready or interested in taking over, and you do not want to sell to a third party. In this case, it isn't about getting that "bigger engine" but of keeping the current one running until a new one can be installed.

For some families, the alternate route is to hire an external professional interim CEO. Hiring an experienced outside interim CEO has three major benefits:

a. It offers fresh eyes to see opportunities, restructuring needs or productivity improvement.

b. Outside CEOs can mentor and develop the next generation of internal successors with less family "baggage."

c. The company can be true to the exit plan of the owners.

This route has unique hazards, as many professional ex-CEOs will tell you. They list these as owners never really turning over the reins; meddling family boards; vague accountability due to unclear milestones and objectives, e.g., financial and succession development targets; the exiting owner continuing to manage key relationships with customers/clients, suppliers, and internal thought leaders.

Because of these hazards, this alternate route needs to have the following conditions for success:

a. Clear family/board support for the strategy and its compensation plan

b. Robust hiring and review processes with clear goals and milestones

c. A well laid-out transition plan for owner's handoffs

d. An investment and timeline for successor development and a contingency plan if none succeed

If "Needing a Bigger Engine," means you feel the challenge of growth, that is a good problem to have! If it means abandoning exit plans to avoid handing over the reins or dealing with inner fears about your future, then it is a powerful road hazard requiring your attention.

Road Hazard: Make the Tough Calls

An important consideration when planning your exit involves the "people" side of your business. The CEO of a successful privately held electronics company shared what he believed contributed to the growth and salability of his company. "It was moving people out that was a key factor, not just developing top talent; it was recognizing the people problems and taking action." From his perspective, the top contributor was making the tough people decisions, which was the foundation of the company's culture of performance. Similarly, the founder of an engineering consulting partnership said his biggest lesson in preparing for his buyout involved addressing partner issues early. "If there are tough decisions to be made you have to make them and move on."

This road hazard is not having a bad partner or weak senior team. The hazard is confusing loyalty to the person with making a tough decision that is important to your company's future.

Intuitively, you know when there is trust among your leaders the work takes less effort. Trust also makes it easier to give feedback and reduces interpersonal conflict. When you develop trust by dealing with issues constructively and early, it allows you to work through serious performance issues that may arise later, even when discussing termination. The more we avoid addressing tough issues, the deeper the hole, the higher the resentment, the greater the erosion of trust, and the longer and more expensive the resolution process.

Alternate Route

Route 1 - Commit to Action: Recognizing issues and conflicts in performance, values or strategy isn't usually difficult. *Addressing* and *resolving* them is.

First, you must determine what your stomach can tolerate. If you are seriously con-flict-averse or emotionally invested (as with a family member), you need the help of a facilitator, mediator, or outside legal counsel.

Second, you need to define the consequences of *not* addressing the issues clearly. The consequence of failing to act could be that you fail to grow due to strategy disagreements, or you lose your best people who cannot continue to work under a weak leader, or *your* credibility as a leader is hurt when your people see loyalty overcoming business intelligence.

Third, you have to understand your options and rights, both legally and morally, and know what is congruent with your company and personal values. What do the buy-sell or shareholder agreements state? What are the company's values including standards of accountability?

Finally, you must be clear about your relationship goals. One senior partner of a professional services firm stated that preserving a 30-year history of friendship with a terminating partner was *as* important as the financial package and non-compete terms of the departure. That goal defined the process (engaging a counselor, not a lawyer) and the measure of a good outcome. It did not change the decision to exit the partner.

Route 2 - Proactive Honest Feedback: Being proactive means having a review process with three main characteristics:

The *what* you review is a) a <u>set</u> of factors that are clear, known and observable, for example performance against results b) interpersonal skills and c) fit with and promotion of the company values.

The review and feedback *process* is simple, frequent and constructive vs. ad hoc and intermittent or only crisis centered.

The people involved are *committed* to doing it well and with a bias for candor and development.

At our firm, we set company performance goals and partners' targets each year. We had formal closed-door partner-to-partner feedback sessions mid- and year-end on results and personal development goals. Topics were sometimes hard to discuss and comments difficult to hear. Did they strengthen our teamwork and help resolve issues? Yes. Did we ever have to overcome our loyalty to a great person and make the tough decision to let him or her go? Also a yes.

Shared visions and values, performance expectations and review processes support addressing and resolving conflict before irreconcilable differences occur. When those differences do occur, then operating and buy-sell agreements or contracts that are clear and up-to-date provide a known structure for making those tough decisions.

Even with attention to prevention, cutting ties is often the best option. Knowing what to do in the interest of the business is sometimes painful. Having the courage and wisdom to do it well is the leadership challenge we all face as business owners. As John Wayne put it, *"Courage is being scared to death ... and saddling up anyway."*[23]

In Conclusion

In this first step of the Exit journey you were asked to commit to the trip. That started with taking a bit of an inner journey to understand your aspirations for your business and yourself. That work explored the perceptions of different generations and how understanding those unique views can help you understand how to market to them. You also explored your desired legacy, the difference you want to have made in your company and your community or industry. And finally, you examined the typical road hazards that owners encounter and some of the alternate routes. If you had a camera in hand you might have taken the snap shots below.

COMMIT TO THE TRIP

Small business owners are a large and powerful group. Different generations of owners have unique perspectives that influence how they approach selling and buying a company. Know your power and perspective.

Exit planning starts with the legacy you want to leave and your goals for the end game. Devote time for life reflection — focus on accomplishments and aspirations. This is as important as figuring out your sales strategy and price.

To achieve your goals, be aware of potential hazards. It's possible to mitigate hazards and create alternative routes to "Too Busy to Leave. Too Tired to Stay," "A Bigger Engine," or "Confusing Loyalty with Business."

SCENIC OVERLOOK

BUILDING INSIGHT AND FINDING MEANING

Scenic Overlooks are a chance to stop the day-to-day driving, pull off the road and think about where you have been and where you are going next. Here you can apply what you have been reading to your situation and gain new insight into yourself and your business.

This first Overlook explores the influence of your underlying values, beliefs and hopes on your exit plan priorities. You might use one or several of the activities to clarify your thinking. The choices here are similar to the results you get when your phone searches for places to eat after a long drive. Some of the search results better fit your mood, dining preferences and what you're hungry for. In an Overlook you what activity is a fit and how you want to work: alone or not, over time or in a single sitting. Skipping the work, like skipping meals, is not a healthy option.

As they say on the airlines, "Turn off all electronic devices with an on-off switch." In other words, find a quiet place to do Overlook work. Here are some suggestions for how to engage in these Overlook activities.

Imagine you are talking to someone you really trust, admire or love. What would you tell them knowing what you say doesn't have to be perfectly formed, and they won't judge you?

OR,

Using a computer, tablet, whiteboard or just paper, fill the page(s) "stream of consciousness style" with the keywords that come to mind – no sentences required – just words (or images!) that capture what you are feeling, seeing or thinking.

I. VALUES DRIVE CHOICES AND OUTCOMES

*Your beliefs become your thoughts, Your thoughts
become your words, Your words become your actions, Your actions
become your habits, Your habits become your values,
Your values become your destiny.*

Mahatma Gandhi

A. Clarifying Values

Explore your values and their implications for your goals. See how the lists you make for any or all of these topics sheds light on defining your "end game." You might complete this individually, with co-owners or a significant other and compare results as a discussion starter.

---

1. My top FIVE values

a.

b.

c.

d.

e.

---

2. How do these values "show up" in my behavior, e.g., if I value candor/honesty?

---

3. What are the implications of these values on how I plan for exiting the business:

Example: Candor and honest

| *How it shows up:* I make my thinking explicit; I don't waffle or avoid tough issues; I'm known for straight talk. I don't tolerate "yes men". | *Implications:* I need to have equally candid and strong exit advisors to help me face reality and difficult choices. |

B. Imagining Turning Over the Keys

Imagine the end state of this phase of your career, i.e., as the owner/leader of this business:

1. What do you see as you turn the keys over?

2. What are you proudest of about yourself, your results?

3. What difference did building this business and delivering its goods or services make and to whom?

4. What, if anything, is difficult to think about or answer at this point in time? (That's ok; it may become easier as you continue on the Exit Signs journey.

II. IMAGINING THE END STATE AND BEING FULLFILLED

A. Reflecting on Your Life History

Life Line: In your life, what have been turning points that brought you to where you are today? Write them on a time line from birth to now. You can use words or drawing/icons.

Some may be high points, a scholarship, promotion or birth of a child. Others may be low points, losing a parent or mate, a business failure or job loss.

- Are there any themes in your highs or lows?
- Think about how these events or experiences influenced your thinking, your direction, and the choices made in your life. What lessons did you take from these events? In hindsight, which lessons served you well, which did not?
- Since the past (behaviors and lessons derived) can be a predictor of future behavior and choices, how does this life line analysis shed any light on how you want to approach exit planning or the next phase of your life?

III. RANKING YOUR SELLING PRIORITIES

When you are planning your exit, it is crucial you understand your goals and priorities. If you don't know what's important to you regarding your business and your life, you'll be driving blindly into an unknown future. By letting chance have the wheel, you and your employees may end up somewhere you'd rather not be.

On the following page is an example of how to clarify goals and priorities. The statements are from an owner of a medical practice based on conversations about what he was trying to accomplish in the sale of his business. His ratings clarified his thinking and illustrated how the business had changed over time. His wife completed the exercise, too. Their discussion about their answers allowed them to align their thinking and priorities.

You should tailor this list to your business, values and objectives by listing the conditions you hope to meet in the sale of your business. Then, force rank them through a distribution of 100 points to the objectives that MOST express what you value when you think about leaving your business. At least one statement should have 25 points.

Example

	Rating
My patients/clients/customers are well cared for after I leave; they have quality care and feel valued.	____
My staff is well treated and is free from concern for their future.	____
My retirement (lifestyle and obligations) is more financially secure.	____
My estate is enhanced so I can provide for the next generation.	____
My obligations as an owner are finished; I have freedom from mental stress.	____
I am able to continue to influence the operation and reputation of my practice, e.g., I am able to mentor and support the new owner.	____
I feel I will have left a legacy for others to continue and build upon, either in my business or my industry.	____
I am positioned in my industry to remain active and engaged, e.g., in teaching, advising or as a public speaker/consultant.	____
I have an ongoing income stream from the business over the next ____ years.	____

Reflection:

Who else's view about these objectives and values do you need – partners, significant others/spouses, clients?

Who might you discuss your rankings with that could help you define the implications, e.g., financial advisors, legal counsel, brokers?

IV. ROAD HAZARDS AND ALTERNATE ROUTES

A. Too Busy to Leave, Too Tired to Stay

What keeps you "too busy" and "too tired"?

- First, consider what you are doing that is truly value-added activity for the effective operation of your business.
- Then assess which activities could be reduced, eliminated or delegated. The template below provides a framework to examine five categories of activities that fill your days often mindlessly. Record the work that keeps you busy in each space below.
- Finally, see if you can find 25 percent of them to reduce, eliminate or delegate?

The categories are the most common drivers of work tasks, things you require of others and thing others think they "must have" from you. For example,

- do you require weekly written status updates? Do they really result in re-direction? What is their value and what information do you really need by what means?
- do you have more than one level of approval for low cost expenses or more than two levels for high dollar items? How often is a decision reversed or money truly misspent?

How can you and others reduce work that keeps you in the too busy trap?

Things I generate or require			
What others require of me			

Reports   **Approvals**   **My Habits**   **People**

What I can stop doing:	
Where I can reduce the frequency:	
Who else could do this?	

B. Bigger Engine: Hooks, Hazards and Multiple Options

If you are considering delaying your departure, investigate what is at work behind this plan.

Write down your and others' thinking then discuss the logic, values and emotions at play.

The Hook:

The Hazard:

Other reasonable options:

What advisors should be consulted?

C. Making the Tough Call

Is there a difficult situation that requires a tough call in order for you to move forward with your exit plan and getting your company ready for sale? The following analysis will help you step back and get clarity on your situation.

Name the Player:
Describe the central questions involved:

Consequences if not resolved:
To the Business

To People, e.g., morale

To key relationships

Your Goals for Resolution:
Relationship ◄─────────────────────────► Business
Draw an X where you would you put your priority between keeping/strengthening the relationships involved and achieving a business need?

Describe your criteria for a reasonable resolution, i.e., it must achieve what?

Your Options:
Whether you have a tough call about a person or a business issue, e.g., close an office or buy out a partner, you have several options for action. What are the pros and cons of the options below?

Decide and Tell	Collaborative Problem Solving	Legal Action	Other
+			
−			

STEP 2 ~ MAP YOUR DESTINATION

I have had dreams, and I've had nightmares.
I overcame the nightmares because of my dreams.

Jonas Salk

What is the most important factor in your retirement plans? For most owners, it's financial freedom. The sale of your business will provide the basis for financial security whether as a lump sum or ongoing income stream.

With financial freedom being so important, how can it be that having a plan ensuring it is next to last on many owners' to-do lists? While the average business owner spends eighty hours a year developing an annual operations plan, thereby ensuring *this* year's revenues, they spend less than eight hours a year on exit planning providing for their *future* livelihood and security and that of their heirs.[24]

The main reason business owners give for not engaging in exit planning is, "It's too early."[25] The evidence, however, screams NOT TRUE. The number of business owners who are 70 years old or older has been growing at a staggering rate. Up until 2005, the historical rate of business owners turning 70 was relatively stable at around 20 thousand per year. By 2015, that number had increased tremendously to over 120 thousand per year, a 600% increase! And over the next 10 years that number will further increase to over 180 thousand per year, an increase of over 900% over the historical rate – and it continues to grow until 2030.

Think of it this way. If you <u>knew</u> that the number of homes coming on the market in your neighborhood was going to increase at the same alarming rate just mentioned, and you were counting on your home equity to fund a big part of your retirement, would you say "It's too early" to plan a sales strategy? Or would you start <u>now</u> to get the house in shape to ensure the highest sales price and to downsize well before there was a glut of homes on the market?

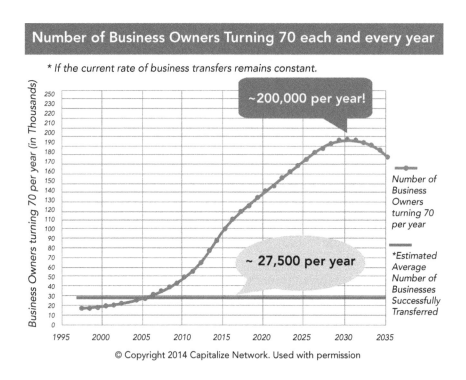

© Copyright 2014 Capitalize Network. Used with permission

Similarly, what if you <u>knew</u> that in your neighborhood only 25-30 percent of homeowners successfully sold their homes (for example for full price and in 30 days) and that this statistic had been true for decades? Wouldn't you think about what you could do to be one of the successful few who sell at top value?

The data above foreshadows the same story for your business. Historically, approximately 27,500 businesses successfully transfer ownership a year (about 25 to 30 percent in the 2010 market.) But in five or ten years the number of businesses for sale will be counted in the millions. Ask yourself, given the rapidly increasing business inventory projected, how long can I put off planning and still achieve my financial goals? Isn't it inevitable, that the prices of businesses sold in the coming years will drop perhaps by half or possibly even more?

Is it really "too early?" and are you willing to risk your retirement by delaying your exit planning with the biggest asset you have? You can no longer wait to prepare your business and yourself for the transfer of ownership. The time is NOW.

DECLARE YOUR PERSONAL GOALS, BUSINESS OBJECTIVES AND TIMING

Let's begin planning with your *goals and objectives*. Goals include your desired financial status, lifestyle and pursuits, estate plans and even what you hope for your employees after you leave. Your advisors can help you by specifying the questions for each of their specialized areas of planning. In some cases, they can provide the analytics and the criteria to be considered, such as tax implications, actuarial data or economic forecasts. Only you can define your objectives, however, which is about hopes and concerns as well as about financial analyses. Take the time to write your initial thoughts to the following questions. They will guide the conversation with your family and advisors.

 ASK YOURSELF

- Why do you want to exit this business?
- How committed are you to selling?
- What is your desired departure date?
- What are your top three goals for the business?
- Do you know what your cash flow needs are to achieve the post-departure lifestyle?
- What are your goals for your employees after you transition?
- What role, if any, would you see for yourself in the business after you leave?

Timing is Everything – What's Yours?

It was at a holiday party where my former CPA declared I had won the "best timing award" for selling my business. It didn't seem like a prize-worthy event until I learned how difficult it seems to be for most business owners to time their exit.

Many, when questioned about timing the sale of their businesses, offer vague rules of thumb. "Get out when you can." "Sell it at the victory lap." "Read the writing on the wall." "You will feel it when the time is right."

However, comments like the following were mixed in. "We knew we couldn't keep up the growth curve and survive (as humans), so we had to put a plan in place that would allow us to be salable in five years." "I keep a close relationship with the investment bankers, so I know at any time the six to eight potential companies that are most likely to buy us." "I could see a limited future for us. We had to plan for our sale three to five years out." Finally, the president of a professional services firm admitted, "I'm tired. When I leave in five years, we will need new blood, new ideas and energy to run a company twice the size we are now."

These two sets of comments separate those with lousy timing and those with great timing – foggy and reactive versus clear and proactive. Too many owners are ambivalent about leaving; choosing instead to believe that there will be a "sign" to indicate the right time.

Advance planning and positioning of your company allows you to optimize timing and eliminate the stress of not knowing your exit date. Ideally, you should plan on a three to five-year horizon to your departure; two years is a *minimum* to realizing your goals.

 ASK YOURSELF

- What is the forecast for your *industry* or *technology*? What do the experts say? What does your gut tell you?
- What is your No Delusions forecast for your company's value and salability within your market/industry in two years? Three years? Four years?
- What current data keeps you up-to-date on the market and potential buyers for your business?
- What is your energy level, physical and mental? Is it fading or stable? What's going to be required of you to continue growing and preparing to sell your business?
- What do you know, or suspect, are the hopes of the significant others in your life regarding the timing of selling your business?

Exit planning is like any highway journey; it's *dynamic*. It can have adrenalin-driven moments and mind numbing tedium. Sometimes you are in the fast lane and at other times, a traffic jam; there are fixed stopping points, detours and GPS recalculations. The important thing is to know your destination and estimated time of arrival and to keep moving forward.

The Scenic Overlook that follows this chapter will help you look in-depth at your intentions, aspirations, timing and motivations as you begin the exit journey.

The Sale is Not the End Point

"May you live a long and prosper" is no longer just a familiar Star Trek quote. A 1946-born baby who retired in 2011 can expect to live about 18 or 19 more years, about 25 percent longer than their parents lived.[26] Men can expect to live to be 82.2 years old; women to be 84.9. While it's exciting to consider how these "added" years could be lived, it also creates a financial challenge. Longevity can be great – if you plan for it.

Like the majority of business owners, you are likely counting on proceeds from selling your business to secure your future. Without advance exit planning, however, that security is jeopardized. It's urgent you discuss a) with your financial planner how to ensure income for a healthy and prosperous life for 20 to 30 years post-exit and b) with your advisory team how to increase the value and salability of your company so that you are at the top of the large pyramid of companies that will be available when you put your company up for sale.

And, sometimes, opportunity knocks, as it did for one fortunate business owner. He received a letter of inquiry from a broker representing a large corporation. Then the tough work began. How should the proceeds be managed? What should he do with his life now? His new best friend became his investment advisor. Despite his obvious good fortune, this owner wished he had thought more about what comes after much earlier.

Selling your business may produce a sizeable amount of money you will not likely generate again. Given this, you must determine:

a. How it will be managed, by what principals and to what ends.

b. How it will be invested so it is aligned with your appetite for risk and your goals regarding, for example, philanthropy or preservation of principal for future generations, liquidity for new life experiences or an avocation that might now be a startup venture.

c. What your monthly/yearly income needs will be, especially as they relate to health and long-term care needs.

In your success as a business owner, you are used to making plans from cash flows to capital investments. Your patience, long view, and sound analytics made these plans useful. Now it's time to think of your Exit Strategy as just another of these long range planning endeavors calling upon your aptitudes and tools.

Despite its left-brain focus, exit planning does have an irrational side. A financial advisor shared a story of a business owner who was a model for planning and working the details of a plan. He refused, however, to have a conversation about an estate plan regarding his business, "after I'm gone." Another couple in their 60s spent months, and many dollars putting a complete financial and estate plan together, yet could not execute the documents on the day of signing. Both the business owner and couple could not deal with the end game despite knowing it was the prudent thing to do.

Secure your future by preparing the necessary financial and estate documents to support their goal. Don't be part of the 65 percent of owners who do NOT have a strategy to pull their money out of their company, or the 62 percent who do NOT have buy-sell agreements to define the rules. Of those who do have documents in place, they are still at risk because the documents are often out of date. The average number of years a buy-sell agreement or an estate plan is updated is over 12 years![27]

Don't let these statistics and stories provide the excuse, "I'm no worse than most people!" Review your exposure and alleviate risk by working with your advisors to ensure you have plans in place. By doing so, you are, as a financial planner described it – helping to move from the baby you love to the life you love.

SELECT YOUR PIT CREW OF TECHNICAL ADVISORS

In our cars today, we depend on a set of displays and warning lights to monitor basic functions and tell us when attention is needed. These indicator lights may motivate some of us to do our own simple maintenance, such as changing the oil, giving us the satisfaction of staying hands-on. However, we also have to rely on specialists to maintain those computerized and inaccessible systems. The same is true for the technical complexity and specialized knowledge needed when selling a business.

Business owners should not expect to be experts in specialty areas. Nor should they expect the knowledge to reside in a single advisor. Technicalities drive wise owners to form teams of advisors with a team leader.

Some of the technical work with advisors occurs far in advance of your business exit, such as drafting estate plans or legal entity operating and buy-sell agreements. Other work occurs during the year or two before ownership transfer such as valuations, asset transfer plans and buyer profiles.

My rule of thumb was always get the best help ~~money can buy~~ for your money. It is true that advisors are not cheap: there are accountants and lawyers and brokers and estate planners, etc. However, not using their expertise can be even more costly. How do you weigh the costs of buying help vs. not using help or just avoiding the whole process of exit planning? Some financial colleagues put the following example together to illustrate the impact of using advisors to help you develop and execute an exit plan vs. DIY.[28]

Let's assume your company is an engineering company with $6,000,000 in annual revenue, 30 employees and a healthy EBITDA of 15%. To the right buyer, a valuation of 12x EBITDA or $10,800,000 is possible. Let's also say that like all companies, yours has a few weak spots: inconsistent revenue and EBITDA, inconsistent or incomplete financial data, management bench strength a little weak below you, and your tax strategy hasn't been optimized for the sale or on operations. The chart below shows the net after-tax proceeds comparing having a transition exit plan vs. having no plan.

Impact on the Bottom Line: With or Without a Transition Plan*

Issue	Deal Killer?	Impact	Hit to Purchase Price	With Transition Plan to Fix Issues
Starting Point			$10,800,000	$10,800,000
Marginal Mgm't Team	Possibly	Reduce multiple 1x	-$ 900,000 11x	0
Inconsistent EBITDA	Possibly, if highly inconsistent	Reduce multiple 1x	-$ 900,000 10x	0
Financials Inconsistent	No	EBITDA by $40,000	-$ 400,000 10x	0
Tax Strategy Not Optimized	Possibly, if net proceeds too low	e.g., Current Tax on Sale 39.6% but could be 23.8%	~ -$ 3,400,000	~ -$ 2,600,000
Total			$ 5,200,000 Net After-Tax	$ 8,200,000 Net After-Tax

© Copyright 2014 Capitalize Network LLC. Used with Permission
*Sale to Outside 3rd Party (Strategic Buyer)

Ask yourself as you examine the table:
- How would I feel if I left 36 percent of the company value on the table?
- How many advisory dollars would I invest to reduce or eliminate that lost value?
- If I go it alone, do I have the expertise in every area required to recapture this value?
- How many more months or years would it take me *without* help (hint – generally twice as long or more) to capture the full value; and what might happen to the market prices of companies, especially given the wave of companies that will come on the market, during that delay?

Think of an Exit Planning advisory team as a Pit Crew at a top NASCAR race. Each member of the crew performs a unique specialty, yet together each creates the results needed from the pit stop. They are experts at that task and the teamwork required to deliver incredibly important results. Likewise, your advisory team must work in concert to help you build the strongest executable plan and help you realize maximum value for your company. Remembering the chart above: you might ask, what is the return you might expect from the investment in advisory service fees? For every thousand dollars you spend will you see an impact on the net after tax proceeds?

Your Exit Planning advisory team should consist of several (but not always all) of the following specialists. The table below illustrates the expertise you might require and their value in planning. In the next Scenic Overlook, you will find a worksheet to help you determine who should be on your pit crew.

Field	Specialists	Technical Backgrounds
Finance	Accountant/CPA, Financial Planner, Estate Planner, Investment Banker	Financial analysis-audit, tax planning, valuation techniques, benefit and compensation plans (employee incentive plans, qualified and non-qualified-deferred compensation) legal entity structures, business continuity planning
Legal	Business, Corporate or Tax Lawyer	Buy-sell agreements, operating agreements, legal entity structure options and related tax law, legal audit (e.g., contracts) business continuity implications for estate planning
Business Sales	Sales Brokers, Valuation Experts, and Small Business Advisors (e.g., Financial Services Advisories)	Business valuation, market analysis, web based and network technologies, forward-looking marketing analysis, buyer lists
Exit Planning	Full-service advisory resulting in a finished plan/roadmap and implementation plan	Multi-disciplinary and project/team management: finance, operations, legal, I.P. and HR.
Organization Effectiveness and Change	Organization Development Consultants and some senior HR Specialists	Succession planning, communications, facilitation

As with Pit Crews who have a Crew Chief, you need a master coordinator – above the fray evaluating every situation, monitoring progress, defining the schedule and next steps. You are the crew chief for your business with your full focus on performance, operations, customers and products. Your Exit Crew Chief has experience in the process of preparing and executing an exit strategy. The Chief builds the teamwork and coordination of advisors performing the myriad of tasks that execute your exit strategy. The Chief is the project manager and the coach of the pit crew and to you, the owner, making sure your internal business data is protected yet available to the project team that you are informed regularly of progress, and that trust and communication are there to meet your goals in your time frame. Whether your plan calls for a third party buyer or an ESOP or LBO, the Crew Chief is your lead advisor there to guide the process, help preserve your sanity and enable you to focus on how to strengthen and grow your business.

Your task is to a) define who you need on your advisory team and who will be the Crew Chief, b) provide them with autonomy and coordination and c) make clear one overriding ground rule in working together: everyone must ask the hard questions and actively listen to understand and learn from each other.

Like a Pit Crew, your advisors must have autonomy but also work together to help you build the strongest executable plan. That means they need:

a. To know your long term goals and your timeline for your exit

b. To know their roles and your expectations for how they work together and with you

c. The freedom to use their expertise with clear accountability for delivering solutions that meet your goals, schedule and budget

The collaboration ground rule prevents advisors from falling into one of two roles. There is the "pair of hands" role where they find ways to support your under-informed thinking, or they play "the only expert in the room" role whereby they beat you about the head with options and advocacy of "what works best" versus deciding together what works best. This ground rule will drive your advisors to explore, analyze, challenge and be challenged.

When coordinated effort does not happen, time and money are wasted as the next example demonstrates.

The owner of a medical practice had his attorney draft a sales agreement based on a one-on-one meeting. The owner then took the sales agreement to his CPA who declared it, "Totally wrong" based on the CPA's understanding of the owner's financial picture. The lawyer was maximizing for the owners' tax and liability exposure, the CPA for cash flow and a quick sale. Rather than put the two of them together to find the optimal solution, the frustrated owner abandoned his lawyer to prevent any more "wasted money." The sales deal failed despite many months of discussions about terms.

How do you prepare your advisors? It starts with completing the Scenic Overlook exercises to prepare your thinking. A good first step is to bring your advisors together for an initial meeting so advisors can meet each other, define the timeline for completing a plan and clarify what they need from you to provide their best advice. In lieu of a kick-off meeting, an owner can appoint a "crew chief" to coordinate communication and the work of the individual advisors. Unless you have the time to do this launch meeting, a crew chief is essential.

There is one expert you will use who is already on the payroll, YOU. Only you can answer the questions that further the strategy work begun in the Commit to the Trip and Map Your Destination chapters.

Key Hiring Decision: To Broker or Not to Broker

You have a fundamental decision to make at this point in your exit plan. Should you market the business on your own or use an external resource? If you choose an external resource, it will either be a broker, if you are a business with less than half a million in assets, or a mergers and acquisitions firm (M&A), if you are a larger entity or an entity with several operating divisions. It's helpful to understand the differences between using a broker and going it alone.

Brokers and Mergers & Acquisitions Agents (M&A)

Brokers and M&A agents represent you and your company to the market and prospective buyers. Their fiduciary obligation is to you. Both can provide expertise on sales in your industry, the buyer pool and valuation and pricing. They handle the paperwork and keep the process on track. They both locate and present you with multiple, qualified buyers either through a private search or advertising.

Some of these firms also work with you on preparing the financials and legal paperwork and with assessing improvement areas to increase the value of your business.

They are your objective advisor and help manage the predictable emotional aspects of the selling process such as demands for broader due-diligence access or disagreements over valuation or terms and conditions.

They both have fee structures. Brokers usually charge a percent of the sale price paid upon a successful close. M&A agents are retained with the monthly fees discounted from the final back-end fee upon a close.

For Sale by Owner

Marketing your own business is no easy task. Only 10 percent of listed businesses were sold in the period between 2005 and 2007. Still, the majority of micro and small businesses are sold without a broker, most of which are mom and pop retail, restaurants or small medical practices.

There are benefits to being your own broker. You are the most qualified expert on your business and can represent its history and current condition with conviction. There are no commissions or back-end fees although there will be advertising costs or listing fees on a private business sales site. You will control the pace of the sale by eliminating the delays of a middleman in preparing documentation, making financial arrangements and negotiating with a prospective buyer. You will be doing all that yourself.

A Word about Time and Costs

Selling a business is an intellectually and emotionally challenging, time-intensive process. You have data to collect (not always readily accessible); financial and legal documents to prepare; road show materials to organize and meetings with prospective buyers, all while still running your business.

At least 20 and up to 60 percent of your time and energy in a given quarter will be consumed in this process. This doesn't count the time your advisors will need you.

Finally, don't fall into the trap of expecting knowledge to reside in a single advisor. It's tempting to have your CPA or legal counsel as your only advisor. You trust them; they are already in the budget, and they already have a sense of your business. They are not always, however, experienced in market variables, pricing and competitive benchmarking or the intricacies of business valuation. The result of not using a set of advisors includes the horror stories of sub-optimal pricing, surprise tax bills, delays and owner/buyer conflicts.

 ASK YOURSELF

- How much time and patience do I have to take myself away from running my business to coordinate the work of my advisors for valuation, financial reporting and legal documentation to manage paperwork, marketing, seller due diligence, negotiations and, finally, meeting closing requirements?
- What is the risk to my business performance if I spend 40 to 60 percent of my time on selling my company?
- Am I well informed on the market for my business (buyer pool, demand for like companies, trends in sales pricing and volumes)?
- How objective and unemotional will I likely be in the selling process when dealing with prospective buyers?
- How much money am I willing to spend on the sales process as a percent of my asking price?

Of course, if you have a ready, qualified buyer, the process may have fewer demands on your time and less emotional turmoil. But don't bet on it.

FIND YOUR MOTIVATION: WHY GO THROUGH THE PAIN?

I dislike long road trips. Put me on a plane and in a crazy airport anytime over a car trip. I have to tap into some personal gratification or all I can see is the work – pack and unpack the car, eight hours or more of driving during which, inevitably, we have arguments over whether we are lost (again) and who is at fault for missing the exit.

Exit planning can seem like a meandering road trip with visions of long, complicated or conflict-ridden days and few intermediate rewards. Not surprisingly, the farther away the exit horizon, the less attention owners give to exit planning, which is the reverse of good practice. Of those who do successfully sell their companies, 75 percent wished they had begun preparing for that process much earlier.[29]

What keeps leaders from doing this work? Here is a partial list of reasons; you decide which might explain your reluctance to spend time defining your exit strategy.

a. It takes you away from what you do best, and what energizes you, the work of growing a business. A recent study states, "Owners say that maintaining focus on the growth of their business is a major reason why they have not spent more time on exit planning to-date." [30]

b. Exit planning reminds you of your mortality and taps into fears about getting old or having diminished value. It asks you to look at uncomfortable questions about yourself such as, "Who am I if not my company?" As several executives put it, they felt as if he had gone from being a "Who's Who" to a "Who's That?" [31]

c. There is always tomorrow and the urgent trumps the strategic. Today's crisis and fire could burn down the house so the plan to remodel will have to wait. The engine warning light that says the oil level is critically low will get your attention and cause you to do something. The "service engine soon" light, however, does not raise the same level of anxiety. It's that "soon" word.

d. All of the above

If any or all of the above reasons fit, you will need to work harder to find meaning and remain motivated with your exit planning work. When work has meaning, it fuels effort and eases discomfort. Here are three compelling reasons to start your exit planning now versus later despite any misgivings. Each rationale has its unique and immediate payoff for the over-committed, multi-tasking, focus-on-this-quarter business owner.

Emotional Meaning: Sanity and Peace of Mind

The number one reason private business sales fail to meet their objectives is a lack of planning on the seller's part.[32] We use our precious time to take care of daily events and things that are deemed "urgent." Urgent always trumps strategic, and exit planning is strategic. Further, we become anxious when looking into the future versus into next week's calendar.

For years, psychologists have explained that anxiety and stress are the mind and body telling us we need to take action. When we take action, it increases our sense of control. By making an investment in planning, you lower your stress, gain greater clarity and develop a sense of security knowing you have a map to navigate the journey.

Psychological Meaning: Quieting the Time Wars

The E-Myth Revisited describes three kinds of work and roles necessary to grow a business successfully: the entrepreneur, the manager and the technician.[33] Each role battles for time on the agenda because each believes that what brings value is the same as what they love to do and do well. Unfortunately, this internal battle creates Time Wars.

It is painful to watch a talented and passionate leader or team of leaders at war over how to spend scarce time and attention determining which topics will deliver the most value to the business. A founder-entrepreneur does not give the same weight to the issues of creating infrastructure or processes, such as project management or financial systems as the manager-leader, nor to the resources to support technical wizardry required to realize the next great thing.

There are big saleability consequences from Time Wars. Your exit strategy options are limited when there is nothing to buy because the business is "all about you" and you are leaving. You may have been the entrepreneurial founder and growth maker, but the value also resides in the sustainability of the company. If you don't stop to consider post-departure sustainability, you may never get to depart!

When asked about succession planning, the founder of a $100 million private company felt it was a waste of time because the business was too complicated for anyone to understand but him. A follow-up question then asked, "What if you got hit by a truck?" His reply was, "I guess there would be a lot of people put out on the street."

Rational Meaning: Building an Exit Strategy Brings a Focus on Business Value Drivers

Your exit strategy focuses on value-creation. You already know that attention to customers, operations and people lets you produce revenue and deliver profit. Exit planning looks at those same factors from the perspective of a potential buyer. How does a prospective buyer define value? What is the basis of their decision-making? How would they size up your company against their criteria?

The outcome of a business valuation exercise and a company health check leads to concrete action plans that influence profitability and salability. These plans become part of your management agenda. Exit planning, then, is where the sky (aspiration) meets the road (your yearly operations plan).

If not even ONE of these rationales for investing in exit planning works for you, you might be in the group who say, "I don't believe it. Prove it to me, and I still won't believe it."[34]

In Conclusion

In step two of the Exit journey you started to map your destination by clarifying more specifically your financial goals, objectives and timeline for selling your company. Knowing the market for a business like yours in the time line you envision will help you build your strategy. To do this well you learned you need a great team of advisors and a way to create a coordinated effort. Finally you heard that it's all about finding your motivation to take action. If you had a camera in hand you might have taken the snap shots below.

MAP YOUR DESTINATION

Everyone you work with in exit planning will ask, "What are your goals and objectives of selling?" and "Why now?" To answer these, you have to dedicate the time to think about your financial needs, desired future lifestyle, tax and estate plans and what you want for your employees when you leave.

Knowing your timing means not only knowing your personal hopes, but also the forecast for selling a business like yours in a given time frame. It also means having a strategy to pull your investment out of the business consistent with your goals and your legal operating agreements.

The sale is not the end. It is the beginning of the next phase of your life. Find your motivation to plan your exit. Is it peace of mind in having a plan? Is it having a solid project plan for what to improve to maximize your profit? Whatever it is, start the journey and stay the course.

You will need expert help. Define your advisory team and a Crew Chief; and prepare them to work collaboratively in your interest.

SCENIC OVERLOOK

SETTING THE COURSE

This Overlook provides four activities to help you build insight into exiting your business. 1) A set of questions about your personal objectives; 2) questions to help define your time; 3) a template for identifying your advisory team; and 4) an example agenda should you bring your team together to launch your strategy work.

When you complete this Overlook you should have greater clarity about who you want to help you build and implement your exit plan; what your 'end game' might be, and what questions you still need to work on such as financial objectives or timeline.

I. CLARIFYING PERSONAL OBJECTIVES FOR YOUR EXIT STRATEGY

In focusing on *goals and objectives* specifically, you are answering the central questions that guide your discussions with your advisory team. Take the time to write your thoughts down.

1. Why do you want to exit this business? What pulls? What pushes? What holds you?

2. Are you committed to selling? Will you dedicate the time and energy needed to make the business ready and plan and conduct the sales process?

3. What are your top three goals for the business, i.e., what would you want to see achieved before you leave? Some examples include growth, operational improvements and talent development.

4. What do you envision as your post-departure lifestyle? Do you want to travel, never have to work again, engage in a non-profit venture, spend extended time with family at a second home, participate on one or more boards, etc.?

5. What will your cash flow needs be to achieve your desired post-departure lifestyle?

6. What are your goals for your employees after you transition? What role, if any, would you see yourself in post-departure?

II. TIMING IS EVERYTHING – WHAT'S YOURS?

Increase insight into your exit timing by thinking about the following questions. The first three questions are a reality check on your business; the second three are about YOU.

By addressing these questions, you will know two important things: what's clear and what's still foggy in your thinking/knowledge and the actions you need to begin now to keep you in the driver's seat and on pace to reach your finish line.

1. What is the economic forecast for your industry or technology? What do the experts say and what does your gut tell you?

2. What is your 'No Delusions' forecast for your *company's value and salability* within your market/industry in two, three and four years?

3. What current data informs you about the market and potential buyers for your business?

4. Is your energy level (physical and mental) fading or stable? What's going to be required of you to a) continue to grow your company and b) prepare and sell your it?

5. What is your ideal time-line to exit? Will you cut the strings or phase out? Will you cash out or earnout? What are other options available to you?

6. What do you know (or suspect) are the hopes of the significant others in your life regarding the timing of selling and leaving your business?

III. WHO IS YOUR ADVISORY TEAM?

This list is a menu of who you might want to advise you depending on the size and complexity of your business, its ownership structure and an owner's estate. Whom do you have or need to have on your team? What are the most pressing issues to address with each/all of them?

Field Name	Specialists specialist Place a ✔	Technical Backgrounds	Issues or Question for this Advisor
Finance _____ _____ _____	Accountant/CPA Financial Planner Estate Planner Investment Banker	Financial analysis–audit, tax planning, valuation techniques, benefit and compensation plans (employee incentive plans, qualified and non-qualified-deferred compensation) legal entity structures, business continuity planning	
Legal _____	Business, Corporate or Tax Lawyer	Buy-sell agreements, operating agreements, legal entity structure options and related tax law, legal audit (e.g., contracts) business continuity implications for estate planning	
Business Sales _____	Sales Brokers, Valuation Experts, and Small Business Advisors (e.g., Financial Services Advisories)	Business valuation, market analysis, web based and network technologies, forward-looking marketing analysis, buyer lists	
Exit Planning & Crew Chief _____	Full-service advisory resulting in a finished plan/roadmap and implementation plan	Multi-disciplinary and project/team management: finance, operations, legal, I.P. and HR.	
Organization Effectiveness and Change _____	Organization Development Consultant HR Specialist	Succession planning, communications, facilitation	

A. Sample Agenda for Advisory Team Kickoff Meeting

Even if you tend to avoid meetings like the plague, the following agenda can make a launch meeting easier. It can also be a guide for individual one-on-one meetings with advisors. This launch meeting is NOT a strategy formulation meeting but a "how we want to work together" meeting to get a great exit strategy defined.

Purpose of Meeting

The purpose of the meeting is two-fold:

1. To launch a team of advisors, so they have an initial understanding of your goals, timeline and the most important exit planning issues

2. To clarify roles and to coordinate what information they will need to assist you in exit planning

Topic	Desired Outcome	Time
Purpose and Introductions	Everyone credentialed and on the same page	5-10 min
Your initial thinking about your exit: hopes and goals, timelines, biggest concerns/ questions	You talk about your goals and your most pressing questions on exit planning for their *mutual* understanding, NOT problem solving	20 min
Coordination and role clarification	Each member give his or her view of their work area, critical needs including data, access, communication and coordination of effort	20 min
An initial timeline	What are the key milestones and first next steps?	10-15 min
Summary	What you learned/appreciated and what was agreed upon	5 min

STEP 3 ~ CHECK YOUR DASHBOARD INDICATORS

The first responsibility of a leader is to define reality...

Max Dupree, former CEO of Herman Miller

The best business owners know how their business is performing. They use dashboard-like gauges to monitor financial, customer and operational performance that are objective and quantifiable. These are one view of reality, but they don't show the whole picture about the value or sustainability of a business and its readiness for sale. When I see the typical check lists I recall Jack Welch, the former CEO General Electric, repeatedly tell his leaders, "Face reality as it is, not as it was, or as you wish it to be." Your reality goes beyond the numbers.

You need another set of gauges to detect the *organizational health* of your business and its *readiness for sale*. These gauges are like your car dashboard devices in that they tell you the condition of systems that affect performance, safety and comfort. These gauges alert you to the performance, value and salability of your company. A client preparing for his exit put it this way, "The operational, legal and tax reviews we did (to prepare our exit strategy) were pretty much of a proforma nature. The information in our organizational health profile turned out to be at the top of the list in importance for what was in our way."

SET YOUR ORGANIZATIONAL HEALTH GAUGES

1. **Culture/Values** and **2. Vision/Strategy** indicate where you are headed and what it means to be a member of your company – the company identity. They are your compass.

3. **Technical** and **Management Talent** are needed to fuel performance. This is your fuel gauge.

4. **Execution Discipline** allows a company to switch gears quickly in response to customer, technology, market or regulatory demands. It is like a tachometer displaying engine load and running efficiency.

5. **Core Business Processes** work to convert the scarce resources of your company into synchronized, forward motion. You need a 'check engine light' to monitor these several systems and alert you when one isn't performing well.

6. **Team Relationships** – can run cool, warm or hot. How comfortable is it to be in those seats? This is like your seat warmer switch.

Six Organizational Health Gauges for a Sustainable and Salable Business					
Culture and Values	Strategy and Vision	Talent: Technical and Management	Execution Discipline	Core Business Processes	Leadership Team Relationships

Here is a description of the six gauges and the questions you should be asking to focus your leadership attention on your company sustainability and salability.

Gauge 1. Culture and Values

All companies have a *culture* that is shaped by its leaders. Leaders influence and direct company culture in several ways. This is done namely by what they attend to, what they measure and reward, whom they promote, what information and authority they share and with whom they share it.

Culture determines people's sense of identity and loyalty, standards of performance and even their response to a crisis or an opportunity like your exit and the sale of the company. They are also the guardrails of your company during the transition to new owners.

Cultures can drift over time, and not all remain functional or healthy. You must have a way to gauge the power of today's cultural on your exit strategy and the transition to new ownership. Know the culture and values, *in practice*, at your company for they not only affect *today's* performance, innovation and talent retention but your company sale value.

Significance for Your Exit Planning

When you realistically portray your company culture and values, you can leverage their value as enablers of performance and sustainability. You can also judge the best-fit buyer for your company that will work and reinforce the culture, not force a major change.

The ultimate implication for you is the power of culture to determine your legacy and the ongoing viability of your company after your departure – two of your three goals in selling your business. Culture fit is the *number one reason acquisitions fail*. This statistic has been true for over 35 years of study.

 ASK YOURSELF

- Can you describe your company culture and values in practice (versus what is printed in company brochures or on posters)? Do your people share the same view?
- Have you included *culture fit* in your due diligence of a prospective buyer? If not, you risk not achieving your post departure goals for profit, sustainability and legacy.

Gauge 2. Strategy and Vision

To position a healthy company for sale, you need a vision and strategy that is clear and known by your people *and* potential buyers. There are two significant benefits to a clear and known strategy. First, your people know the basis for your decisions about, for example, budgets, direction changes or improvement initiatives. Having shared knowledge speeds execution because they can take independent action without micro-management from you. Second, when a third party buyer sees a clear vision and strategy, they can see the fit with their strategy and the assumptions behind your growth projections.

Buyers (and your company leaders!) want to know the answers to these four questions:

- In what competitive space do you operate? Examples include lowest cost, customized solutions and cutting edge technology. In what markets do you operate?
- How are you positioned to win? In other words, what are your core competencies and how are they leveraged?
- What are your goals for the next three to five years? Consider growth, profit, market share, product line and technology goals.
- How does selling your business fit with the company strategy and vision? Be prepared to describe your strategy to prospective buyers no matter the size of your company.

Whether a medical practice, consulting firm or 600-person manufacturing business, these basic strategy questions apply to you! You don't need a formal strategic planning process to answer them, but you do need clear answers.

Significance for Your Exit Planning

As an owner, you are the compass carrier and map maker. The more clarity in your map, the more likely you get to your destination. What happens when the heading is not clear or the compass is not regularly read – as when different leaders within a business have just slightly different bearings for the destination? In nature, hikers following a bearing that is just one degree off can translate into almost 100 feet of error after just one mile. That means that after a five-mile hike, they may miss their target by almost five hundred feet, which may not sound like much unless it dumps you off a cliff.

When the leaders in your company do not know, agree or understand the strategy and vision, they have difficulty leading confidently or feeling ownership. They will unconsciously portray these things to prospective buyers, which can create doubt in bench strength. When your leaders are under-informed about strategy, they predictably wonder about their role in the company's future, especially once it is known that you are looking for a buyer.

Let's be clear though. If you urgently need to sell your business in less than a year, don't spend time creating a vision and multi-year strategy. In this scenario, your tasks are about executing on three *tactical* objectives: cleaning up the financials and documenting results, defining the selling plan that guides terms and conditions and finding a buyer. Your fast-cycle exit plan has the primary objective of cashing out, not leaving a legacy or driving sustainability.

If you have an exit horizon of two years or more and are focused on the goals of profit, legacy and company sustainability, ask yourself:

 ASK YOURSELF

- Are you providing the compass headings for your business and your exit?
- Who knows the vision and strategy? Who doesn't but should? Are your leaders all on the same map and heading so they can act independently yet in concert?
- How engaged have potential successors been in either shaping the vision or translating it into a strategy for execution, so they feel ownership?
- Is there a review system that tracks progress on your business and Exit strategy, and are reviews on your calendar?

Gauge 3. Technical and Management Talent

Bench strength is usually listed in the top three to five factors external buyers look at in determining the value of a company. Buyers hesitate to purchase companies where they don't see strong leaders behind the owner. Family businesses don't beat the odds of surviving to a second or third generation without strong successors.

Key talent development builds a strong bench, but it requires a long-range horizon and an investment of an owner's time and attention. According to Ken Blanchard, leaders have three options for having great talent: hire a winner, hire a potential winner and develop them or pray. Are you praying your future leaders become winners or are you supporting them with the information, authority, job assignments and coaching that fosters growth?

Significance for Your Exit Planning

Leaders who see retention as a priority ask, "What are we doing with our key talent?" Without development, the path to a leadership (or an ownership) position may feel, for a high-potential successor, like being blindfolded in a car's front passenger seat. It may be obvious to your key talent that they are moving ahead. They hear you talk about how great it is to have them on the ride. But that blindfold represents the lack of a plan and the essential coaching they need to see their place in the future, to build their capability and responsibility and to feel an integral part of the journey.

I worked with a professional services firm that believed it had exceptional bench strength. They also hoped to exit one of the founders within 18 months. However, in talking with partners' direct reports, little had been done to prepare them to come off the bench although they had been nicely rewarded for good work. It was not until a real star among the group said, "Boss I have an offer from another company…" that the owners saw a serious threat to their exit plan and felt a sense of urgency for a systematic development process.

When you want to improve the salability of your company, you need a realistic evaluation of your technical and management talent to show the capability for sustained results after your departure.

 ASK YOURSELF

- How well are you paying attention to developing bench strength? Is it seen as a priority and on the management agenda versus an ad hoc activity?
- Are your best people, especially potential successors, engaged in setting goals for their careers and learning?
- Have you completed a talent profile with the value contribution of key people and the company's obligations and associated costs? Build it into your company prospectus/story.

Gauge 4. Execution Discipline

Execution discipline influences the speed, costs, results and morale of your company. It can make your company look like a finely engineered car or a clunker. If a prospective buyer spent a day watching people at work in your organization, would they see your people *over-revved* with too many priorities or projects or *in idle* waiting for decisions stalled in reviews or debates? Would they see a company lugging the engine by using antiquated processes or operating at maximum efficiency?

To assess execution discipline, look at five areas.[36]

1. **Decision Making:** The ability to make the right decisions quickly with a level of acceptance that drives action.
2. **Speed:** The ability to be faster at translating ideas and analyzing issues as well as responding to information AND ambiguity.
3. **Accountability:** The capability to have *reasonably* unambiguous clarity of roles, spans of control, priorities and expectations. It means having *transparency* of information, progress, issue resolution and consequences.
4. **Delivery Integrity:** The capacity to sustain alignment, focus and coordination around priority issues, which must be delivered to satisfy key constituents such as customers.
5. **Performance Culture:** The desire to and practice of harnessing every brain in the company to generate, work through and learn from the best ideas, regardless of origin, and then execute with urgency.

I recently worked with a mid-size company executive team looking for a merger partner. They were frustrated with the progress made on simple initiatives, so we did a simple execution discipline assessment. They learned there was a pattern of weak accountability – unclear roles, fuzzy expectations and deliverables – and inconsistent delivery integrity. They lacked consistent coordination and focus on priorities and timelines. These patterns affected product development and commercialization, two competencies critical to a prospective merger partner in their industry.

I also worked with a growing environmental technology company. The two owners were planning to retire within 18 months and sell their ownership shares to internal talent. Their plan was threatened by a lack of execution discipline, slow executive decision-making and a performance culture that was sub-optimum. People consistently said, "We don't make decisions around here." The owners were busy being technical experts working with clients, and *did not delegate decisions*. Important issues rose to the top where they stalled until the leaders were together (rarely). Fortunately, the people delivered superb projects, but *only* they felt the pain; the owners were in the dark.

Weak execution costs money and reduces speed. It also erodes morale, confidence and loyalty at a time when you are counting on the next generation of talent to take over the business.

Significance for Your Exit Planning

When you work on strengthening your execution discipline, the salability of your company will grow. Its company value will increase because buyers will see scalability and feel confident there will be little need for post-close investments of time or money to improve execution.

 ## ASK YOURSELF (OR YOUR PEOPLE)

- What kind of effort does it take to get something done around here?
- How are your people engaged in improving the discipline of execution? Do they feel listened to?
- How many and what kind of decisions are stalled at the top? What does it take to get a decision made at your company, both from your view and your employees'?
- What might a potential buyer see or hear about the speed at which your company can adapt to opportunities or external challenges?
- Would a buyer see your company as a high-performance engine or a clunker?

Gauge 5. Core Business Processes

Processes enable or cripple a business. They are conveniently invisible until they are thrust in our faces when they don't work. Everything we do *in* a business is part of a process even if we detest the thought of working *on* a process. When I mention the word "process" to business owners, you would think I was their significant other demanding we have a talk about our relationship. Many business owners just don't <u>do</u> process work. Others win awards and price premiums <u>because</u> they do.

No business process is cost-free, but an ineffective one is always expensive whether in dollar terms or human frustration and motivation as the following example illustrates.

This mid-size company had experienced double-digit growth for most of its 15 years; product lines and the complexity of assembly had all grown. Each department manager had created procedures, processes and related software systems to fit their needs. At one point, there were 17 different systems for staffing and line loading. The result was a) the huge cost of maintaining 17 unique legacy systems and b) increasing reaction times to changes in production volumes because of the difficulty of moving personnel across shifts, lines or products. The cost of operations jeopardized private equity financing for planned growth.

Significance for Your Exit Planning

Your goal is to build a sustainable company and leave a legacy of mature and simple business processes. This leaves the buyer confident that costs are controlled, quality is built in and the business won't require large management time post close.

You know that process performance affects profit, resilience and salability. You know that time spent improving a process is as much an investment in your business as new IT systems, the latest mobile phones or spending time hiring that bright new expert. You need to know what makes your processes perform effectively and efficiently, and to identify and take actions that make a difference in the bottom line and the value of your company.

ASK YOURSELF (OR YOUR PEOPLE)

- Where is the greatest waste in *how* work is done, e.g., time, money, materials?
- Where do redundancies exist, and where could best practices be migrated to other areas?
- How do your customers experience your company from sales through product performance to billing or service error recovery? Your prospective buyers will explore this to understand the roots of operating costs, warranty liabilities and reputation.
- If you stood in the shoes of a potential buyer, where would you see the biggest opportunities for process improvements?

Later in Step 6, you will further explore how to assess your process health and its impact on people and salability.

Gauge 6. Team Relationships

Nothing is as exhausting on a long road trip as conflict, chaos and communication problems among passengers. Everything takes longer from deciding where to stop for food to debates on the best route. The same applies to a family or team of company owners. A long history together, issues of loyalty and entitlement, and people's skills make getting to the desired destination more difficult.

A poorly functioning management team makes transferring ownership difficult for owners. It is emotionally draining and time-consuming to reach agreements on valuation, terms and timing when there are long-standing, unresolved management team problems. When I asked a company president what had been the easiest aspect of putting his exit plan in place he said, "Nothing was easy about it when you have personalities, which means having living, breathing partners."

Investors, strategic partners and third party buyers think twice about investing in companies with weak or dysfunctional management teams. They know they affect the performance at lower levels in organizations. When owners or senior leaders set up functional or hierarchical fortresses with moats, their people don't usually build bridges. In other words, prospective buyers can bet money that the good, the bad and the ugly stuff they observe in the lower rungs of an organization were passed down the ladder.

I have had the privilege of working with a CEO in two of his emerging-company ventures. One of his consistent goals was to build a foundation of trust and foster mutual respect as he built his diverse, senior team. He knew this would enable them to constructively lead the company through its growth and eventual sale. The ability of this CEO to build a high functioning team was part of his stellar reputation in the industry and made his companies attractive to investment partners and eventual buyers.

Leadership values and practices like these are especially important in family businesses. Families that spend time building teamwork while working together are more likely to have multi-generation successors. I interviewed the family patriarch of a successful greeting card company who had a lot to say about the importance of fostering respect and trust in his management team, all of whom were his children. He and his adult children believed the secret was in how they were raised as kids, were involved in the company and allowed to find their individual passions within the business. "Dad groomed us kids to work together as a team and to respect each other, to talk openly about our dreams and seek common ground.... He allowed us to both fail on small scales and to succeed on large ones. We always knew we were trusted and what that meant."

The toughest scenario is when trust has eroded. There are typically two causes: the foundations for healthy conflict are missing, thus conflict escalates or becomes chronic; or truly covert action has occurred that damages the business and the relationships within it. I have worked with both situations; while the first instance is uncomfortable, it is fixable. The second scenario is also resolvable, but usually involves expensive lawyers.

Significance for Your Exit Planning

Whether you are a team of unrelated officers or a multi-generational family, building solid, productive and warm relationships is a deliberate and thoughtful process requiring an investment of your time and energy.

ASK YOURSELF

- What is the level of trust and respect within my team (or the family) *and* the behaviors or practices contributing to it? Is it enabling or limiting our company's performance?
- What are the consequences our existing relationships in implementing my exit plans?
- Do I have the 1) motivation to be vulnerable and open to learning and changing what my part is in the health of your team and 2) the skill and detachment from the dynamics of my team or family to work through the resolution process?

Asking these questions requires a strong spine and commitment to personal growth. I have never seen a leadership team where the person at the top was not some part of the problem and, therefore, part of the solution – i.e., had to make personal changes. Have the wisdom to call in an outside consultant to support building, repairing or reconfiguring your team relationships and effectiveness.

CONDUCT A DASHBOARD REALITY CHECK

If you use the six gauges as an assessment device, they tell you what to pay attention to, where to allocate resources and how you might engage people in the process of improving the value and salability of your business.

Should you do such an assessment before a business valuation or after? If it's done before, you can identify obstacles to a high valuation and pinpoint value-enhancing projects. As with selling a car, you assess its condition, correct deficiencies and highlight its best features. You want it to qualify as "excellent condition" in the blue book valuation table.

If the assessment is done after a valuation, you can define which deficiencies or strengths will likely cause a decrease in assessed value. Since most owners overestimate the value of their company and are disappointed by the buyer's valuation, having *The Number* first and seeing the detractors, may generate more urgency and motivation for improvement initiatives.

Either way, facing reality by doing a health and readiness assessment tells you what time it will take to strengthen the business before putting it on the market. Tuning up a business in Step 4 can take anywhere from one month for a simple fix to well over two years for implementing major growth plans.

You might conduct a health assessment in the following ways.

- Owners conduct a self-assessment knowing that those at the top have only one perspective on the organization.
- Interview a cross-section of your people using the six gauges as guides for the questions. This requires a brave and impartial internal staff person to collect, categorize and present the confidential picture. An alternative is to conduct a survey using SurveyMonkey® or another online survey tool for the same purpose.
- Use an external organization development consultant to collect data and generate a profile. This often comes closest to describing what an external buyer would learn in their due diligence.

A review is only as good as the meaning and action it promotes to making a company *market ready*. Owners with a market ready *mindset* know what the top three critical areas to remedy are in the months ahead and have a plan of execution, and they monitor improvement plans. They have assessed:

Operationally: How sound are the financial accounting and reporting systems, intellectual property protections, performance data, and market forecasts? How current are supplier, employee and customer contracts? What are the human resource weak spots or issues, e.g., compensation, benefits or other historical and future costs?

Organizationally: What positively and negatively impacts the transfer of ownership? What processes are inconsistent or inefficient? Does the culture foster collaboration, speed of decision-making and innovation? Is there a succession plan?

Salability: What improvement plans will build a strong company story for the strategic as well as financial buyer so that a prospective buyer will see the value beyond the numbers?

Some business owners question where to find the time to do a readiness assessment while running the day-to-day. Others believe they have no choice but to start. Still others will say, "Thanks, but can I get back to what I am more comfortable doing now?" In the first and second groups, leaders should look for the low hanging fruit that will provide some early momentum. As for the last group, this quote from W. Edwards Deming seems appropriate, *"It is not necessary to change. Survival is not mandatory."*

Facing Reality: A Leadership Case Study

The following is a case study to illustrate how owners face reality and then define priorities. These include, what they will attend to, why they are legitimate priorities and where they might engage their talent. The case is an *aggregate* story of two companies in order to better illustrate the tool and their resulting leadership priorities. The companies were successful, cash-positive and had over 10 years of steady growth. Both were defining exit plans for one or more owners.

As you read through the illustration and analysis, think about your company and ask these questions.

- What would you be glad to see and what would most concern you?
- What would you put on your leadership agenda given your exit strategy?
- What might be your people engagement strategy for working the most important transitions?

The graphic illustration here portrays the main themes from company interviews organized around the six dashboard indicators of organizational health. Of course, there were extensive examples from interviews to explain the themes, which were presented at a leadership meeting.

The Case Context

These were companies with many strengths and a history of success. They had the talent, the commitment and solid reputations for performance. Their growth, however, disguised many hidden problems, and as the U.S. economy weakened, their weaknesses were amplified. Profit and future growth were at risk at the very time when the owners were on their final laps to their exit finish line.

Using the six gauges of organizational health as a visual framework, this is what their reality check showed. The first box under the health factor listed the shared interviewees' perspectives on the company *strengths such as* "Strong Implicit Values" or "Founder's Energy." The box or boxes in red describe the *weaknesses* people saw, such as "Lack of Clarity" around direction or "Support for Development."

Culture and Values

Strong Implicit Values
#1 Growth
#2 Client relationships
#3 Delivery integrity
#4 Technical smarts
#5 Autonomy of work

Values in Question*
#6 Innovation and risk-taking
#7 Accountability

*Are these "for real" and do all owners believe these?

Strategy and Vision

Founder's Energy Inspires

Lack Of Clarity
#1 What is our direction and who knows it?
2. Little Alignment on:
- Direction i.e. where to play; how to win in the LONG run?
- Growth ~ how much, how fast?

Strategic Planning
We don't spend time planning; it takes away from selling and doing

Talent: Technical and Management

Exceptional People
"We hire people who like to take it, figure it out, and run with it." Partners' skills are exceptional and specialized. Reputation with customers is exceptional.

Support for Development
1. Need more transfer of client relationships to non-owners.
2. Less ad hoc development of the next generation.
3. Give us tools/methods that enable delegation of responsibility

Core Business Processes

Process Aware
1. Strong Staff Desire for improvements
2. Best-practices exist and ready for migration

Low Process Maturity
1. Little migration of best practices.
2. Redundant processes and systems.

Execution Discipline

Weak Execution Discipline
1. Weak Operating Cycle to plan and monitor; has a triage approach to problems.
2. Few mechanisms for managing, project budget reporting, resource planning.
3. *"We don't make crisp decisions."*

Low Process Maturity
1. Little migration of best practices.
2. Redundant processes and systems.

Leadership Team Relationships

Strong Loyalty to the Business and Clients

Enduring Conflict and Eroding Trust
1. Frayed relationships from failure to follow through on commitments or reconcile conflict over "unequal effort."

Analysis

In the analysis of the interview themes, three stakeholder perspectives are important.

- What is the meaning of the data for the *current owners?*
- What would be important if the prospective buyer were an *external buyer* (individual or company)?
- What would be significant to a potential *internal buyer/successor?*

Significance for the current internal senior team: The top three **strengths** they recognized and wanted to reinforce were:

1. A performance culture that valued delivering results for customers.
2. Keeping exceptional technical talent who were proud of their contribution and felt positively challenged. This was a competitive advantage in their industry.
3. An engaged staff able to lead operations improvements to make work less frustrating and who had a shared sense of urgency.

Note to you: These are value-enhancing attributes of this company. As such, they belong in the company story or selling memo with the supporting data such as on time delivery of projects and services, customer satisfaction and key talent profiles. Be sure you use assessment strengths into your company story.

The partners identified three top **issues** affecting their exit goals as well as the growth of the business.

1. There had been inadequate attention to successor development, especially sharing responsibility for key customer relationships and defining the path to ownership for key employees. This was an urgent priority. Departures of high potential leaders would affect both customers and staff morale.
2. They saw a strong need for simple operating systems to provide information for managing projects and profitability.
3. They heard a loud cry for more knowledge and alignment on strategy and vision among the leadership team and with key talent.

Significance to potential external buyers: The assessment is similar to what a prospective buyer tries to discover in their due diligence. It's better that owners should uncover and claim the strengths and mitigate the issues than have outsiders report them. The owners believed that <u>buyers'</u> priority issues would center around two red flags:

1. A "hub and spoke" management style with over-dependence on the senior partners to carry the customer relationships. While most acquisitions by larger companies mean that owners will be replaced either immediately or within a year, the risk to do so is the potential loss of key customers and projects. It could be a showstopper.
2. A potential loss of key talent could occur from a lack of clarity about the future and their frustration with managing projects. The new owner's transition challenge would be to retain key talent – sharing the vision of the new owners, discussing career objectives and perhaps engaging them in transition planning, thus demonstrating their confidence and value in them.

Significant to potential internal owners: The partners felt that the issues for internal successors were similar to those of the partners: strategy, development of successors and operational improvements. Moving forward key talent wanted to see:

1. Identification of successors and greater authority and accountability for improving the management processes and for owning customers;
2. Partners moving out of the way and distributing power and responsibility; i.e. to see a path out of the *founders' trap* defined as, "What got me here won't get me there." Owners had to show that they could be to be less engaged in the technical work e.g., sales, engineering and their analytical specialties, and do more to mentor successors and lead change.

The question I asked owners was, "When the economy turns around, what will happen if you do nothing about what you learned here?" In other words, would they be transition leaders or go back to being workers? Would they continue to *attend* to the issues affecting their exit and consistently *engage* and develop others? With a two-year exit horizon, they had plenty of time to make the company ready for the transfer.

SET YOUR PRIORITY TRANSITION PLANS

Frankly, the findings in a readiness check are seldom a surprise. After all, you experience much of your company strengths and weaknesses daily, but when presented as six simple gauges affecting your readiness to sell, you can focus. The transition priorities for your leadership agenda become clearer, whether they are about process, succession or strategic clarity. How to *lead* those transitions is discussed further in Step 7 of the exit journey.

In Conclusion

Step 3 broadened the set of dashboard gauges you should be using to understand the performance of your business and its readiness for sale. These include: culture, vision, talent, execution discipline, business processes and team relationships. It provided an example of how assessing your readiness can clarify priorities for improvement through the eyes of the buyer as well as the owner.

CHECK YOUR DASHBOARD INDICATORS

You know how your business is performing financially, on sales and customer satisfaction. You also need to know how to evaluate organizational factors that influence value and salability.

Each factor affects your business performance and its value and will impact how quickly your company is ready to be put on the market.

Assess the organizational factors – tout your strengths and correct the weaknesses. Your prospective buyers will evaluate these factors, so be proactive.

SCENIC OVERLOOK

CHECKING REALITY TOOLS

This Overlook asks you to examine your company's readiness for sale and uncover the traps you might encounter in this leadership work. There are three activities to assist you in this examination:

Activity 1 is a set of survey questions for the six gauges of organizational health. You might use this as a discussion guide or collect individual ratings in advance and show the findings for a management discussion. If you are a sole owner, then the discussion might be with a trusted advisor, manager or family member.

Activity 2 is a summary sheet for turning your discussion of ratings into a visual graph of highs and lows. This is for those who like using a concrete number. Don't be fooled, though, it is just as subjective as open-ended questions.

The goal is not to agree on individual rating per se, but to agree on where there are strengths and where improvements are needed to enhance the value of the company. The output should be a set of priority action areas with accountability assigned for a plan and its execution.

I. FACING REALITY ABOUT ORGANIZATIONAL HEALTH

A. Survey Tool

Directions:

1. Review the definitions of the six Organizational Health Gauges.
2. Answer the 24 questions below as an individual or include your senior team in completing the survey. Do note that gathering information this way does lack a broad perspective. Others' perspectives can be gathered via simple on-line survey devices such as SurveyMonkey® or with an external consultant conducting interviews and presenting the findings.
3. Discuss your answers with your co-owners or executive team to identify strengths and weaknesses. This might be done one section at a time at a series of management meetings. Use the Summary Sheet that follows if you want to translate the discussion into a rating' profile. This is not meant to be a scientific survey, but a way to hold an important ownership discussion about the reality of your company's readiness for sale.
4. Define any priority improvement areas that will affect performance, value or sustainability of the company.

Culture and Values

1. The behaviors and practices that exemplify our beliefs and values in practice are

2. The practice we most need to change because it constrains our future is

3. The stories and anecdotes people tell about our company (or me or the ownership team/family) suggest we hold the following beliefs and values

4. The core values of our company could be described to a potential buyer/partner as these three:

Vision and Strategy

5. What is our/my vision or aspiration for the future; what will we become and to what purpose?

6. Have we defined a strategy for the next phase of our business, e.g., where to play, how to win?

7. How aligned is my ownership group/family on a vision and strategy? How satisfied am I with this?

8. Who in our company could articulate our vision and/or our strategy? Who needs to articulate it but can't? What are the implications of this?

Talent management

9. The path to ownership (if internal transfer is an option) is clear to potential successors. It is

10. The three main criteria for successor leadership positions in the company are

11. We have identified the top 5 to 10% of our talent needed to assure our future. Some of their names are:

12. I/we have a process for defining and monitoring the development needs of our top technical and leadership people in the following ways:

Execution Discipline

13. The area of greatest strength for our company, as we execute with discipline is Decision Making, Speed, Accountability, Delivery Integrity or Performance Culture. I know this because:

14. Our greatest weakness in execution discipline is

    The evidence is:

15. People would describe our decision-making as

16. People would describe their ability to influence change and improvement as

Core Business Processes

17. Our five to seven core business processes are

18. The metrics we use to understand the performance of our core processes are

19. The processes that most affect our customers are

20. The "owners" or "champions" of our top core processes are:

Team Relationships (or Family Relationships)

21. The three words I would use to describe my leadership team/partners, etc., are

22. The examples of our team's working style are

23. The one area where we could improve as a leadership team is

24. When working with my partners/team, I most avoid discussing/working on because it usually means I/we

B. Facing Reality – Summary Sheet

Given the answers to the 24 questions, you might translate the individual thinking into a ratings graph. In this discussion, you can quickly see areas of agreement and variation. A caution, ratings are as subjective as qualitative comments. Deriving an average score, or other statistics, may *feel* more scientific, but it does not produce clarity. It is important to guard against judging others' ratings, as in, "How can you only give that a 25?" Only in discussing the rationale for a rating and the variation in the ratings can you gain mutual understanding.

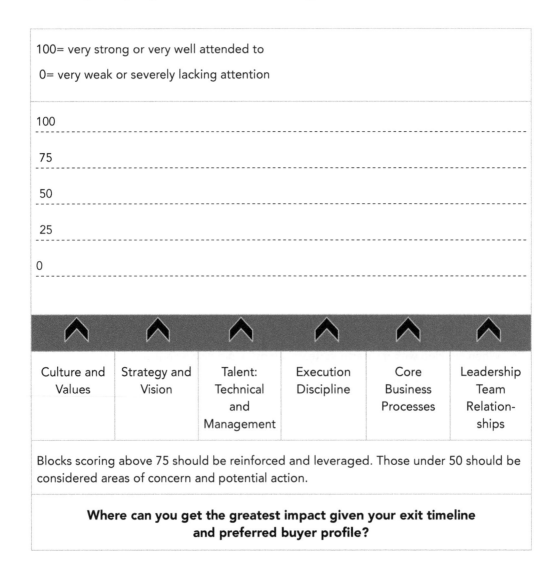

100= very strong or very well attended to

0= very weak or severely lacking attention

| 100 |
| 75 |
| 50 |
| 25 |
| 0 |

| Culture and Values | Strategy and Vision | Talent: Technical and Management | Execution Discipline | Core Business Processes | Leadership Team Relation- ships |

Blocks scoring above 75 should be reinforced and leveraged. Those under 50 should be considered areas of concern and potential action.

Where can you get the greatest impact given your exit timeline and preferred buyer profile?

SECOND LEG

SUSTAINABLE AND READY FOR SALE

Directions

STEP 4. TUNE UP YOUR VALUE AND SALABILITY

Gauge Your Salability

Monitoring Tune-up Plans

SCENIC OVERLOOK: GAUGING SALABILITY AND TRACKING PROGRESS

STEP 5. PUT THE RUBBER ON THE ROAD: VALUATION & BUYERS

Understand the Real Value of Your Business

Declare Who You Want to Buy Your Baby

SCENIC OVERLOOK: REVENUE OPTIONS AND YOUR BUYER PROFILE

STEP 6. SECURE YOUR COMPANY'S SUSTAINABILITY

Mature Your Business Processes

Secure Customers and Revenue Streams

Retain Key Talent

Identify Your Personal Sustainability Path for "Life After"

SCENIC OVERLOOK: SUSTAINABILITY TOOLS

STEP 7. GEAR UP FOR THE SALE

Adjust Your Calendar

Protect Your Interests in the Sales Process

Build a Supporting Data Bank and Data Credibility

Define Sales Process Agreements

Review Company Legal Agreements

SCENIC OVERLOOK: GEARING UP TOOLS

STEP 4 ~ TUNE UP YOUR VALUE AND SALABILITY

You can't build a reputation on what you are going to do.

Henry Ford

When selling your car, you fix it up to improve its salability so you can sell it fast and at a fair price. You look at the major systems to find the weak points affecting value. You also examine what influences the ease and speed with which it will sell such as appearance or maintenance records. In Step 3, you performed a reality check on your company's operational and organizational health to uncover areas where you have strengths and where a tune-up is needed. Step 4 continues that evaluation to assess its salability. There are recognized factors that affect *salability*. Just as there is some overlap in what impacts a car's value and salability, (such as its mileage and appearance) you will see some overlap in factors of operational performance and salability factors, such as good financial records and strong bench strength.

GAUGE YOUR SALABILITY

Salability determines how quickly your business will sell given both external market forces and internal factors unique to a business. You improve salability when you track these six factors.

External Forces Are a Fact of Life

The recession of 2008 through 2011, followed by the 2012 and 2013 government budget sequestration and shutdown, caused huge implications for small business owners. Profits and business confidence plummeted. To exercise control over bottom lines, some owners had to re-route their plans. Systems and facilities upgrades were postponed to preserve cash; hiring was delayed; new store openings were deferred; retirements and the sale of businesses were put on hold.

By 2014, the market for small businesses began improving. Businesses that had managed cash flows, built up balance sheets and improved profits were positioned to benefit from the change in the lending environment as the Small Business Administration (SBA) and banks began slowly funding sales. Valuations went up 15 percent; sales transactions were up 20 percent, and SBA loans were up 25 percent over the previous year. "People who wanted to retire and feel like they missed the boat are absolutely seeing their businesses come back to the point where they're saying they're not going to miss it this time."[37]

These two different economic periods demonstrate that while you are subject to external forces you cannot control, you can mitigate the consequences by focusing on internal salability factors so you can weather the bad times and be well positioned for a strong market. The wave of businesses coming on the market in the next five to ten years is the external force you need to prepare for now.

Internal Factors You Control

You've seen the lists: "21 most important factors in selling your business;" "Eight factors influencing the sale of your business;" and "The four factors that predict sales transactions." They all include, as a rule, the following six factors.

- Growth strategy
- Financial and Operating Efficiencies
- Customer base
- Depth of management
- Assets including product pipelines and intellectual property (I.P.)
- Price and financial terms

Growth Strategy

Nothing sells like growth – past growth, current growth, believable forecasted growth. A growth strategy targets customers, geographies and products/services (new and existing). It includes *organic* growth plans such as innovation, customer concentration, market penetration and/or diversification, and *inorganic* growth plans, like strategic partnerships or mergers and acquisitions.

A recent study of the success factors in growing small businesses found three drivers of small business growth. The fast growth companies always had a) a Profile of their Ideal Customer, b) a Repeat Sales Plan and c) a Marketing Plan and a clear set of Metrics.[38] Companies that have defined their ideal customer profile and then target their marketing to this profile see a 25 percent greater profit and 42 percent greater growth in revenues than those companies that do not have this in the growth strategies. Similarly, those who build a repeat sales plan for existing customers have a 79 percent higher growth rate.

Implications for Your Exit Strategy:

Describing a coherent growth strategy, showing how it has been executed and the results powerful value generators and salability factors.

- Develop and document a growth plan if you don't have one that is holistic, i.e., it includes sales/marketing AND implications for finance, human resources, operations and outlines the threats to growth as well as the opportunities.
- Define a clear and concrete Ideal Customer Profile and Repeat Sales Plan.
- Set out the measures for the plan and how you will monitor it.

Financial and Operating Efficiencies

A new owner of a medical practice said the best advice he heard about buying a business was, "Never buy something you have to fix in the first two years." That may be the mantra of your prospective buyer as well; can they tell what needs fixing and how significant is it?

Some car owners keep a detailed record of every tank of gas, maintenance and parts purchase. Those little books carry great weight with some prospective car buyers. They build confidence in how the car has been cared for and how it will likely perform going forward. Similarly, business financial records affect salability. They must be accurate, complete and provide transparency to instill buyers, lenders' and investors' confidence. The chance of selling is improved 60 to 70 percent when this is true. Likewise, the ratio of selling to asking price will be above the average ratio when an owner has this level of transparency in their reporting.[39]

Thus, accounting practices, operating efficiencies, and process quality must be examined from the view of the buyer. Decisions that made accounting sense to an owner in order to reduce taxes, such as expensing personal cars or carrying an owner loan on the books, will work against valuation and salability. Cost of sales, warrantees, and long lead times may signal to a buyer additional post-close investment vs. a company that is turnkey ready.

Finally, do you know how you rate as a potential acquisition compared to other companies in your industry? Consider benchmarking your business on key financial ratios against peers to learn your strengths and weaknesses. How do you compare on such things as cost of sales, operating expenses and debt on margins and operating cash turns? At our firm, we researched our practices and key ratios for the consulting industry. We learned we were well above 75 percent of firms our size and larger on low operating overhead and high utilization rates and revenues per partner. We could leverage this knowledge when potential merger opportunities arose.

Implications for Your Exit Strategy:

- Assess the state of your *systems and records for completeness, coherence and accuracy*. Prepare well in advance for the due diligence demands of potential buyers, or you will find your valuable time (or cash) consumed in reconstructing history and generating information.
- An item high on your To Do list is to visit your CPA/Chief Accountant to clean up the Balance Sheet and Profit and Loss sheet (P&L). Remove or reduce discretionary spending, scrub out treasured tax write-offs and personal assets, dispose of unproductive assets or unsalable items, which are detractors to a buyer looking for a valuable turnkey asset versus a bargain fixer-upper.
- Conduct an operational audit. Stand in the shoes of a potential buyer observing your business. How current are your financial systems? What are the costs of

rework, recall and warranties, which affects the bottom line and perhaps suggest post sale risk or investment.

- Review contractual obligations and documents to vendors, employees, contractors and financiers. Are they up to date? Where is there financial or legal exposure?

- Review and, if needed, revise your revenue and business models based on benchmarking (and don't forget your intuition).

Customer Base

Customer base is characterized by its *concentration* and *diversity*.

Concentration means two things: having all the revenue eggs in one or two (versus many) baskets or having the owner control the hen (revenue production). Some companies have operating principles that no customer may account for 50 percent of the business. In our firm, we tracked our customer revenue regularly to keep revenue concentration visible and proactively manage the risk to forecasted revenues.

Concentration is also about founder/owner behavior. It isn't unusual for a founder/owner to personally manage over 50 percent of the revenue-producing clients in small companies. In one case, partners feared that the company would forever be known as "John's Company." In our firm, as we added new partners, it was essential that we did two things. First, we made sure that every major client had two partners visible in large engagements and second, we changed our name from "Dennis and Associates" to a name that would build an enduring brand identity.

If you are a product company, you are just as vulnerable to concentration issues. Yes, it's important and cost effective to build long-term relationships and mine existing customers. The danger is that their share of your customer pie makes you vulnerable to changes within the client organization, as when your sponsor leaves or when there are downturns in their industries. This last vulnerability was painfully illustrated in the auto-manufacturing sector as parts suppliers watched their revenues vanish when GM and Chrysler declared Chapter 11 bankruptcy. A concentration of customers and revenues will ring a loud alarm to a potential buyer.

Diversity of your revenue source looks at mix and size of products, lines of business, markets and/or geography. Diversity in your business sources protects you against a downturn in one sector or industry. Early in this millennium, the consulting industry was blindsided when the U.S. markets took a downturn after the high-tech crash. Our competitors and we faced a dwindling demand for external consultants. Fortunately, we had already diversified into natural resource markets and Australia, which allowed us to continue growing. We had to be vigilant, however, that this success didn't create a new concentration problem with the mix of clients or create imbalance in our geographic diversity.

Managing diversity means scanning the external environment for early warning signs of change. It requires you to be strategic and proactive. A useful starting point is to create a simple pie chart of your customer portfolio and update it regularly. You will have a ready story to tell when explaining to a potential buyer how the diversity of revenue sources stabilizes future earnings.

Implications for Your Exit Strategy:
- Establish data-driven measures and methods for making adjustments. Don't rely on owner hunches and anecdotal reviews by sales account leaders.
- Map relationships of owners or account leaders to revenues and customers/key accounts. Where is there a need for dispersing clients to account leaders?
- Stay in touch with your industry associations, small business reports and other thought leaders to monitor the long-term revenue prospects.

Depth of Management

Buyers do not write large checks for businesses that revolve around an indispensable owner who then leaves. They do see a valued asset when there is strong bench strength even when they plan to bring in outside executives. While this should be obvious, owner-centricity is not only common, but also a deadly detractor to a sale. This was discussed earlier in Organizational Health Gauges, and it's reiterated here because depth of management is a big value salability factor.

Lack of depth in management can result in fewer interested buyers, discounted valuation and earn-out terms to protect declining company performance when you leave. This is not always the case, however. While evaluating a potential acquisition, the CEO of a media company found the management level under the selling owner to be quite strong. He agreed to a cash buyout and then offered ownership stock in the combined company to the next level managers.

Since your goals are profit and company sustainability, ask yourself, will your talent profile enable or limit you?

Implications for Your Exit Strategy:

- Profile your best performers and their contribution to the top line. Illustrate succession paths.
- Document employment agreements and buyout or retention bonuses. Calculate any financial obligations and liabilities.

Product Pipelines, Intellectual Property and Physical Assets

Assets are anything of material value or usefulness owned by your business. There are tangible assets (physical and observable) and intangible assets (anything recognizable, non-physical and salable). Inventories, property, cars and equipment are physical and countable; their book value can be defined. But identifying what the intangible assets are in a business and their value often spurs significant debate between seller and buyer (or partners and shareholders transferring ownership shares). A typical list of intangibles might include:

- Intellectual property (IP): trademarks, patents, copyrighted materials, franchises.
- Customer loyalty and customer lists (size of list and reputation of those on it): customers' loyalty is the number one value-creating factor in brand valuation because it provides an even and predictable revenue stream.[40]
- Backlog of orders or long-term contracts.
- Goodwill and brand recognition: few companies have the enviable position of Coca-Cola whose intangible asset value of trademark and brand recognition is greater than all its tangible assets.
- Distribution arrangements, options or favorable leasing arrangements.
- Key talent such as management, scientific, creative, sales or other specialized expertise: when the owner or other key talent produces a significant portion of the innovation, revenues or company profit and leaves because of the sale, a steep key person discount can result.

Bill Gates once said I.P. has, "The shelf life of a banana." Nevertheless, salability of your company is enhanced when intellectual property is a protected asset with a vigorous life expectancy. If your product pipeline is out of sync with patent expirations, for example, its a threat to long-term solvency could trigger an increase in the discount rate applied to the valuation of your business. How well intangible assets and their value are understood (and agreed upon) and then managed, protected and preserved, influences any pricing premium in the sale of your business.

Implications for Your Exit Strategy:

- No matter how significant you believe your company's intellectual property to be, you must be certain you have title to patents. Also, check that all copyrights and trademarks are registered. Finally, document your list of intellectual property.
- Establish metrics to keep the diversity and shelf life of I.P. visible. If product innovation or new lines of service are critical to future growth, determine whether an organic growth plan (perhaps with private equity partners) or an acquisition is the better strategy given your investment capabilities.
- You must be able to convey to prospective buyers a) the value basis of these assets and b) how they are being managed to extend their value over the life of the asset.

Price and Terms

Some might say this is THE factor in business salability, although this view uses a commodity approach to a business sale. Price and terms are the *initial filters* that guide further inquiry, but we know from empirical studies that the strategic objectives of a buyer can trump the power of an initial price review. That is not to say the salability of a company won't be seriously affected if the price relative to revenue or earnings is weak and cannot be justified (for example by above average growth rates and favorable owner financing) or that price and terms will not reduce exposure to potential buyers.

Implications for Your Exit Strategy:

- Spend time on your terms sheet and use your advisors! Consider working with a business broker with access to pricing data, market trends and the ability to create a range of options for terms and conditions that both target and maximize the buyer pool. Employing the assistance of advisors or brokers has two huge advantages: a) advisors will objectively describe the factors effecting your business' valuation and salability by identifying the weaknesses you are likely to miss or excuse; and b) they help you feel confident about your assumptions about the salability and the pricing and terms that align with your objectives. This is explored further in Step 6.

- Be clear on your post-exit financial goals and desired role, tolerance for risk and willingness to provide owner financing. In other words, terms depend on the answers to those personal strategic questions in Step 1.

Caution Sign

This does not exhaust the list of factors affecting salability. Your task is to determine which factors will most influence the profitability (and thus salability) of your business in its unique industry or market and what market forces are influencing the sale of businesses.

Don't mislead yourself about the salability and value of your business. Sometimes you are so exhausted by your work that you can only see problems. Sometimes you are so focused on the price you need to support your retirement or next endeavor you can't see what the numbers are telling you. By going through the work of exit planning, you will be able to evaluate more objectively and present your company with balance and accuracy.

You want to be able, as with selling your car, to write that For Sale by Owner ad. It will likely fall into one of three categories: a) "like new," meaning it has a few cosmetic issues or dings; b) "good condition but needs work," e.g., brakes; or c) "parts only car," where the value is in the parts a buyer may need, leaving them to sell off the rest. Knowing salability issues will allow you to describe its condition accurately to a prospective buyer and focus improvement plans affecting current and future return on investment.

MONITORING TUNE-UP PLANS

Let's be honest. You know that in business, what counts gets measured, and what gets measured gets done. Like that car trip odometer, you need a progress monitor. As you create your tune-up plan, assume a 6- to 18-month horizon to complete the work. Define what must begin and what must be completed by when. Declare how you will measure progress and results.

My mantra has always been measure what matters, not what's easy. There are two kind of measures used to monitor continuity plans. One is an "on-off" measure such as, "implement new budget package." Yes, we want to know if it is being done, but we also want to know if things are working better because of the new budget package. We bought the new package SO THAT our information would be more accurate or complete or timely and SO THAT we could make better decisions based on the information. If you ask the SO THAT question of each tune-up activity, you begin to name the true value of the work to the performance of your business.

Your objective is to create a simple way to easily understand what the improvement priorities are, the difference they should make, how to measure them, and who owns the action. Tracking should be visual and clear just as the dials and readouts on your car dashboard … not lengthy spreadsheets! The value of a dashboard is its focus, simplicity and stimulus for discussion and action. The owner of the tune-up initiative keeps the detail project plan; the owner of the business keeps the dashboard. Your questions should always be:

- Is the deliverable clear and measurable in terms of its impact on your goals?
- Is there clear accountability for who is driving this effort and is it in their yearly performance goals?
- Is there a regular review process on management's calendar?

This is an example of visual dashboard for tracking tune-ups as part of a company exit plan.

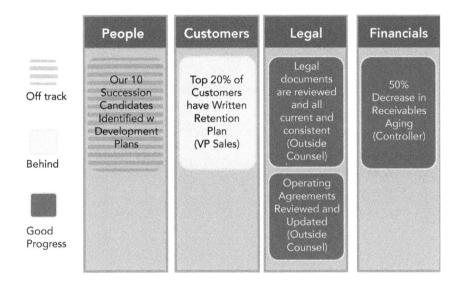

In Conclusion

In Step 4 you examined six controllable aspects of your business that impact salability – from growth to operating efficiencies to management bench strength. Knowing the strengths and salability issues will allow you to prepare your business for a faster sale and represent it well to buyers.

TUNE-UP FOR IMPROVED VALUE AND SALABILITY

Salability determines how quickly your business will sell in your market. You control six internal salability factors: growth plans, operating efficiencies, customer base, assets, price and terms, and depth of management.

Prioritize the list of tune-up items using the full set of gauges: organizational health indicators, financial yardsticks and salability factors.

Set up a process to track tune-up progress including accountabilities, improvement measures and frequency of reviews.

SCENIC OVERLOOK

GAUGING SALABILITY AND TRACKING PROGRESS

Here are three activities to help you gauge your salability and track your progress. The first is a rating sheet you and your advisors might use to plan action where needed. The second is a matrix for prioritizing improvement opportunities. The third is an example template you might use or modify to track the progress of your tune up plan.

When you have completed this Overlook work you will have a better understanding of what salability factors you need to work on with Advisors or staff so they are strong in the eyes of prospective buyers. You will also have a tracking process for improvements you initiate.

I. SALABILITY

A. Take a Reading

Directions: Take a reading for these salability factors. Peg the dial on the gauge from 0 to 100. If it's not where you need it to be, define your action plan to get it there.

Growth Plan

0 = No plan in place

50 = Initiatives in progress

100 = Plan realized

50 / 0 / 100

Action Needed:

Financial Records

0 = Unknown current state

50 = Initiatives in progress

100 = Complete and Auditable

50 / 0 / 100

Action Needed:

Customer Base

0 = Unclear picture

50 = Concentration OR Diversity Improvement plan in place

100 = Both plans are nearly complete and continuously monitored

50 / 0 / 100

Action Needed:

Management Depth and Dispersion

0 = We haven't a reliable picture of our management depth

50 = Our bench strength is good, but not well documented

100 = Our management talent is strong, profiled and protected

50 / 0 / 100

Action Needed:

Assets: I.P., Physical, Product Pipeline

0 = We have no complete and current list of our assets

50 = We have a complete and current list but spotty protection

100 = Our tangible and intangible assets are protected and will clearly extend the life of our company

50 / 0 / 100

Action Needed:

B. Prioritize Your Improvement Opportunities

Pay-Off Matrix

This matrix has been widely used to help leaders prioritize problems and opportunities using two simple criteria: implementation ease and impact on goals. When you have completed your operational, organizational health and salability check-ups, there are always many possible initiatives for growth, efficiencies, value, and salability improvement. The pay-off matrix gives you a structure for prioritizing and aligning on targets knowing what it will take to make an improvement happen in your company environment. And, it's simple to use.

Draw the matrix on a large whiteboard and have a stack of sticky notes.

- Using the sticky notes, write down all the possible improvement ideas -- one issue or opportunity on each note – and place them on the matrix.
- When there is a major disagreement on the location (e.g., quick hit vs. strategic) listen to the perspectives and search for examples/evidence.
- Decide what the top two to three items are that you will sponsor i.e. attend to, resource and engage your people in. Make sure they also include some quick hits to build momentum.

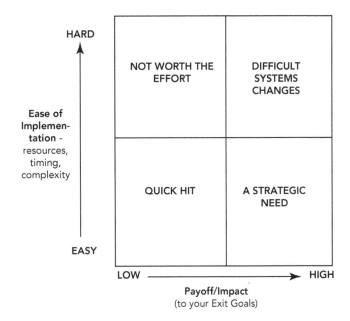

II. MONITORING YOUR TUNE-UP PROGRESS

A. A Visual Management Board

- What are the three key tune-up plans you need to monitor? The three below are only examples.
- Who is the point person for each?
- What are the specific capabilities or outcomes you are targeting in these areas i.e. SO THAT?
- How will you know if they are on track?
- If a plan is off track, what is the plan forward?

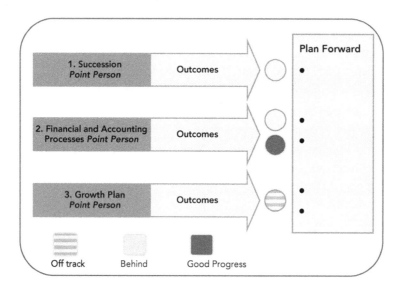

Your Plan Should Consider

a. What project management or tracking systems do you currently use or could adapt to these improvement projects? Avoid creating additional reporting burdens. What do you need as owner, and what do those leading a change project need?

b. What is the review frequency you want to use to track progress and keep it visible?

c. What meetings or other methods might you use to conduct those reviews?

STEP 5 ~ PUT THE RUBBER ON THE ROAD: VALUATION AND BUYERS

A monkey never thinks her baby is ugly.

Haitian Proverb

In Steps 3 and 4, you looked at what drives value and salability. Here in Step 5, you are *calculating* value. This includes deciding what methodology and algorithms you will use, making explicit your assumptions and beliefs about what counts, investigating the market conditions that make this valuation credible and producing a fair price to buyer and seller.

Conventional wisdom might hold that business valuation is a proforma kind of task: fill in the blanks for the five areas above and out pops The Number. It is a mistake to assume that these discussions are simply objective, rational and data-driven. The process of business valuation, while analytically intense, is also an emotion-laden process affecting you, the dynamics within an owner group or family and eventually between owner and potential buyers and successors.

Working through these tasks will answer basic questions about your exit strategy:

- What are the market trends for sales of businesses like yours? What are your assumptions and what is the data? (Never confuse the former with the latter.)
- Given your post-departure goals, what valuation method is best for you?
- What is the ideal buyer profile? What is the size of the buyer pool with that profile? What are your transfer options, e.g., internal versus external buyers?
- How do you wish to transfer business ownership and by what finance mechanism? How do financing and tax strategies optimize your estate and retirement lifestyle interests?

- What are the implications of the answers to the above questions for your current business financial model, legal entity designation and key legal operating documents?
- Bottom line, what are the implications on your personal post-departure goals?

Before you can complete this step, you must come to grips with very personal decisions. What price are you willing to accept, bottom line, for your business? Is it realistic? To answer that you need to have faced the questions in Steps 1, 2 and 3 and worked with your advisors on your strategy. You will use that work here in Step 5. Beware, you need to be open to modifying your previous thinking based on the reality of the analyses and the options they present.

There is little room for error in these areas; working with a team of technical advisors is essential.

UNDERSTAND THE REAL VALUE OF YOUR BUSINESS

Like selling that first car, that you had saved for, you faithfully maintained, and in which you created lasting memories, parting can be bittersweet. Similarly, you have spent the nearly all of your waking hours building and nurturing (on average, 25 years for Boomers) and, in some cases, saving your business. Your baby is beautiful, fabulous and unique – isn't it obvious? Regardless of a few flaws or current *momentary* headaches, your investment of emotion, sweat and capital has been huge. Now it's time to let it go and reap the rewards. First, here are some sobering considerations:

- The average business owner has 75 percent of their net worth tied up in their business, US Department of Commerce reports that only 20% of the businesses that are for sale will successfully transfer ownership.[41]
- Most business owners exit their business with less than six months of advanced planning. Consequently, they receive a mere 50 to 70 percent of the business's potential value.[42]

These figures indicate a very large number of owners will have a disappointing return on their investment or just close their doors.

Calculating Value

It can be difficult to describe what you hope your business will provide when you sell it. It can be also be complicated and emotional when there are multiple owners deciding how to value it. You're not always fully aligned on values, priorities and the bottom line Number. If emotions are ignored or differing views are not explored and made explicit, chronic conflict and weak decisions result. That's why the work in Step 5 is both the analytical and the human.

Here's an example of how assumptions, philosophies and values complicate the valuation process. There are owners who see their business as an income stream to support their lifestyle. Others view their company as an investment with a high, long-term ROI. One perspective is not better or worse than the other, but the differences are critical. Consider the following examples.

Owner A defines his priority as maximizing yearly income, tax write-offs and year-end bonuses including any retirement contributions. He wants to see short-term growth and prefers to minimize long-term investments. This owner, for example, might evaluate staffing for whether it will increase overhead, provide flexibility for current projects and shifting business volumes. He is a minimalist when determining the infrastructure necessary: he feels he only needs a good bookkeeper and a decent spreadsheet to track receivables. Key employees and contract labor don't need employment agreements; nor is legal oversight on contracts or intellectual property a valued expense. This owner sees income growth coming from funding his personal investment portfolio to meet family financial goals. This owner's end game is often to sell the assets and close the business. He may see a market valuation approach as being in his best interest.

Owner B's priority is building equity using very different criteria and metrics. She focuses on revenues and profitability of the business over time and the potential for high returns on investment when the company is sold. This owner asks, for example, how do I budget for marketing and sales to build long-term contracts, or invest in developing intellectual property as part of our growth strategy? How do I ensure I have the people in place to day to lead new lines of business in the next three to five years and to lead the business when I leave? While careful about administrative overhead, she will use advisors to protect assets and to think strategically with her. This owner's equity perspective targets investment in the company for long term revenue and asset growth. She may see using a discounted cash flow valuation in her best interest.

Personal views are important to business valuation, and each of the above scenarios has merit. This is true for three reasons:

- Differing perspectives often reside within the *same* business or family of owners. Coming to an agreement on the value of the business for a buyout or sale will be difficult (but possible). They will need to agree upon how the tax implications of a valuation method are reconciled, what numbers fill the valuation algorithm and what factors to use for predicting future earnings.
- Personal *values* also affect the approach to valuation. An altruistic business owner reduced the objective market valuation of his practice because he wanted to make it affordable to talented young buyers. Another owner would not accept the goodwill calculation believing it was a symbol of greed.
- Buyers have priorities, philosophies and values, too, and they may confound all the great analysis you have done. A former small business owner characterized what he learned about business valuation this way: "You won't ever get the 'true valuation price' because no one else wants to work as hard as you did to make up for the investment."

You are encouraged to consider hard and soft factors when calculating value knowing that your buyer may place a different emphasis on them:

• sales
• brand image
• industry repu-
  tation
• earnings
	• goodwill
	• net book
	  value
	• product pipe-
	  lines
		• customer
		  churn
		• market fore-
		  casts
			• fair market
			  replacement
			  value
			• intellectual
			  property
				• key talent
				  replacement
				  costs
				• management
				• net present
				  value (NPV)
				  rate of money

In truth, all of these approaches produce an *opinion* of the value of a business, which may not be its true value. You might say company value is "What a buyer is willing to pay," but that is too simple. The true *fair* market value of a business is the sale price which a buyer and seller, being similarly informed of the relevant facts, freely agree upon. A seller must know which method produces what valuation and how it affects sales price decisions and salability, and also how it impacts their life goals.

Valuation Methodology

The American Society of Appraisers (ASA), the Institute of Business Appraisers (IBA) and the National Association of Certified Valuation Analysts (NACVA) have defined three major approaches to business valuation. Each approach has several methods to determine business valuation depending upon the business. Here are the basic definitions. This list is not exhaustive; additional valuation methods within each category have been omitted. The optimum approach should include a discussion with your advisors.

Market Approach:

The Market Approach is a valuation method utilizing sales transactional data to predict company value. By looking at sales transactions of similar companies, much like real estate comparables, an estimated value by proxy is determined. As with home valuation, the credibility of the valuation is based on the currency of data and similarity of businesses in the comparison to the business being valued. Privately held businesses are especially difficult to compare given their financial data is seldom published. A good valuation expert can find comparable companies and provide a persuasive argument for a higher value than a buyer might provide.

Income or Discounted Cash Flow Approach:

The Income Approach method converts anticipated economic factors and results, such as earnings and cash flow, into an aggregate, present dollar amount. Thus, income might total after-tax profit, pre-tax profit, EBIT (earnings before interest and taxes), EBITDA (EBIT plus depreciation and amortization), into a single measure of worth. Discounted Cash Flow is the most frequently used and preferred approach to business valuation in particular with businesses of five million dollars or more.

Discounted cash flow seeks to adjust earnings for noncash expenses, such as depreciation or amortization, by subtracting a defined amount for future capital expenditures and any liability payments. This provides a picture of the future projected net cash flow. A purchase price is calculated using present-value concepts for that future cash flow and an estimated discount rate over the period.

Cost or Asset-Based Approach:

This approach determines a company's value by analyzing the market value of its assets. It establishes only a *floor* value since a healthy going concern usually has more value than the liquidation of its assets. The present value of anticipated future cash flows, i.e., *goodwill,* enhances the value. The obvious exception to this situation is a low-margin business, which owns high-value real estate, yet has low future cash flow projections. In this case, an asset-based valuation may exceed the going-concern value. Such a company might be a candidate for liquidation versus sale. In general, an asset-based approach is not the preferred valuation method for service businesses.

Discussions and decisions about valuation are most productive when they are *least* urgent. That means proactively and regularly reviewing: 1) the state of the business, 2) assumptions about salability, 3) valuation methods and data, 4) owner goals and then updating legal entity documents, e.g., Buy-Sell, Operating or Shareholder Agreements. These documents define the commonly held facts and assumptions, conditions, methodologies, algorithms and underlying beliefs for valuation decisions. Make sure they are accurate, current and agreed upon.

 ASK YOURSELF (AND DISCUSS WITH ANY SHAREHOLDERS)

- Do you know the end game goals of each owner? How aligned are you?
- What is your understanding of how your business is to be valued? By what method and data are to be used?
- Who should help you with these valuation decisions and calculations?
- When did the owners and advisors last review the company legal documents?
- What has changed in your business or industry that has implications for these documents and your financial accounting?

The Buyer's Calculation

After doing good work deriving The Number for your business value and generating a price that reflects it, you must contend with the buyer's valuation. Just as with your valuation work, analytics *and* values come into play. It's that "never tell a mother her baby is ugly" moment. You can expect some or all of the following to be true.

Buyers will never feel like you do about your business. While they may appreciate your sweat equity and passion, it will not enter into their valuation.

- They will have aggressive ways of looking at cash flow to anticipate and compensate for errors in calculation or to reduce risks from growth assumptions.
- They may use a different definition of earnings in calculating historical financial performance and goodwill.
- They will be conservative on break-even estimates for their investment especially if they are lifestyle or financial or strategic buyers.
- They will use their own or industry/market data for determining the multiplier on earnings.
- They will question why you are selling and when you decided to sell. They will want to know if this is part of a long-term plan and is it raising a red flag for a buyer trusting performance and forecast data.

Your security is that you have an exit strategy, and this is but one leg of your exit journey. You have taken a hard reality check, tuned up the financial, operations and legal aspects of the business and developed great management bench strength. You are selling a sustainable business of which you are proud.

Remember, the valuation you do drives your expected sales price. The real price will depend upon the same calculation your buyer makes, their values and reasons for buying a business and the economic and market conditions for business sales.

DECLARE WHO YOU WANT TO BUY YOUR BABY

Many a man has fallen in love with a girl in a light so dim
he would not have chosen a suit by it.

Maurice Chevalier

Inevitably, when you think about selling your company, you have to decide how you want to cash out and who your ideal buyer is. The illustration below presents a 10,000-foot view of your basic options knowing that simplicity disguises the complexity of your decision. You will zoom in from this with your advisors or other business owners/leaders to define the unique options for your business. Let's dissect the picture.

Revenue Options

The revenue mechanism defines how sale funds will be generated and from what source: an outright sale, a phased sale or liquidation of assets. Unlike used-car sales, business sales are rarely outright cash transactions. Financing is typically involved whether by an external lender or the seller. Seller financing is involved in up to 90 percent of small business sales and more than half of mid-size sales.[43] A buyer should be willing to consider financing or expect a smaller pool of buyers.

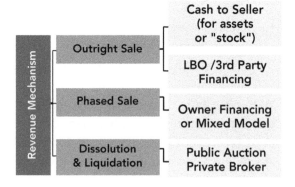

Outright Sale

Most small business owners hope for an outright sale, i.e., to cash out. This is the simplest mechanism; the buyer gets the keys, you get the money. There are two ways to cash out: sell the company's assets or sell your interest in the company, e.g., stock, shares or units. Whether an asset of stock sale is preferable or allowed will depend on your financial goals, tax implications, potential liabilities and the type of legal entity designation: corporation, sole proprietorship, LLC or partnership.

In an asset sale, the buyer is acquiring the physical assets, such as equipment, facilities and customers, as well as intangibles such as patents, intellectual property, trademarks and goodwill. The seller maintains ownership of the legal entity and usually any long-term debt obligations. Asset sales are seldom cash transactions. Many small business sales, including family transfers, are asset sales.

As an owner, you'll want to consider the tax implications. Asset sales can generate higher taxes because tangible and intangible assets, such as goodwill, are taxed at different rates. Similarly, your company's legal entity designation, e.g., C versus S corporation, will affect the taxes you, the seller, will pay. For example, a C Corp is first taxed upon selling the assets to the buyer; the owners are taxed again when the proceeds transfer outside the corporation. If you have recently converted your company from a C to an S corporation, another set of tax rules apply.[44]

In a stock sale, a buyer purchases the seller's shares/interest directly and so owns the legal entity, the assets and liabilities. Whatever assets or liabilities the buyer does not want are either distributed or paid off prior to the sale as part of the terms.

Owners benefit tax-wise in a stock sale because you likely avoid double taxation as proceeds are taxed at a lower capital gains rate and are typically free of future liabilities stemming from product and pension claims or contract disputes, for example. Many stock sales involve a discounted price to compensate for the potential buyer's exposure to the unknown, but a purchase agreement can include clauses that shift the responsibility back to the owner.

Because of these differences, a general rule of thumb is that stock-type sales usually benefit the seller, and asset sales are more beneficial to the buyer.

Phased or Gradual Sale

An entrepreneur sold her successful retail business to one of her vendor representatives with a six-month phase-out of her training and advising involvement in the business, a down payment and a three-year payout on the agreed price with bank financing by the buyer.

A business owner sold his yacht charter business to his son and daughter-in-law with a multi-year buyout. It included that he remain the active captain of the boats for several years while the younger couple "learned and managed the business side." The Captain, i.e., Dad, earned a salary and received yearly payouts. In other words, the yacht charter owner self-financed the sale.

These are examples of phased or gradual sales. The owner agrees to an initial down-payment with a payment plan over time. The financing is from either an external source or the seller.

There are many ways to provide seller financing. For example:

- The buyer makes a down payment with the seller taking a note for the balance.
- A third party, such as a bank or private equity group, provides the funds (mixed model). This is similar to cash out except the payments are phased and may be tied to performance.
- The business entity or a significant asset, such as a building, provides the collateral for the note via a lien filed with the secretary of state's office. If the buyer defaults, the seller takes over the business.

There are advantages and exposures in a gradual sale. A retiring owner has an ongoing stream of revenue from the business without the obligation and effort of running it; and the buyer is able to make the purchase by structuring a long-term payment plan with seller or bank financing. The seller may even be able to expense future payments by creating a consultant retainer for the exiting owner. The exposure to the seller is if the business fails to continue profitably for the duration of the payout. For the buyer, the exposure lies similarly in having paid a price for assets and goodwill plus the interest of servicing the debt with no guarantee that the revenues will endure.

Liquidation

For your exit planning purposes, liquidation is the voluntary decision to discontinue or close a business entity and complete the sale of its assets. It isn't bankruptcy liquidation. Closing and liquidating a business is a tactic that 20 to 30 percent of business owners take. The reasons vary: sometimes it's for want of a buyer; sometimes it's due to a financial or health crisis; and for some it was always their intended exit strategy.

It is not as simple a process as you might imagine. There are legal, financial and tax implications and requirements from filing dissolution documents to canceling registrations and business names to complying with labor laws, to canceling business credit cards and filing a last IRS tax return or K1 for the business. The decision to dissolve and liquidate requires expert assistance whether a sole proprietor, corporation or partnership. Defining what an asset is and its value, if not done well, can leave significant money on the table. In other words, like any exit strategy, it requires a plan. The Small Business Administration website has several pages outlining the considerations and approaches to liquidation and dissolution of a business.

A Critical Lens on Revenue Options: Tax and Estate Planning

You have examined selling options at a macro level so far. We're going to drill down to a critical aspect regarding revenue transfer options, namely, that of taxes and estate plans. You must be able to answer the question, "What sales transaction will produce the optimum tax and wealth transfer benefits appropriate to my unique circumstances and long-term goals?"

No one likes to leave money on the table or unintentionally burden successors. But less than 30 percent of those with succession plans for the sale of their business set up effective tax and estate strategies to accomplish their goals.[45]

Estate planning options are numerous, complex and individualized. The number of variables and considerations to determine what is a viable estate preservation strategy for you requires experts working with you to answer questions such as:

- Would selling your business sooner versus later be advantageous? As capital gains tax increase, an owner has to get a much higher price in later years to net even with a sale at today's tax rates.
- Would selling or giving shares in your business to key employees this year be advantageous? The IRS allows a discount on the value of those shares because

most potential buyers can be reluctant to pay top dollar for the purchase of part of a business.

- Is there an advantage to beginning the transfer of shares of a family-owned business to children now, so that you can take advantage of the current lifetime gift exclusions and current business valuation rates?
- What are the tax implications to you from the various types of external sales versus an Employee Ownership Stock Plan (ESOP)?
- What preplanning techniques exist for each transfer option, e.g., gifting, trusts and limited partnerships for the various options? Which fit your post-exit goals?

Few of us are knowledgeable enough to navigate this part of the journey alone. It is essential that you consult your estate planner and financial advisor to know your options and define your transfer plan. Revisit your plans periodically as your circumstances and U.S. tax policy changes. Be part of that 30 percent who maximize wealth transfer.

Buyer Options

Who might purchase your business (what individual or entity) and from where will they come? There are two main categories of buyer Internal, family, management or other key employees, and External, an outside third party such as a competitor, a strategic partner, a private equity firm or a public offering of stock (IPO).

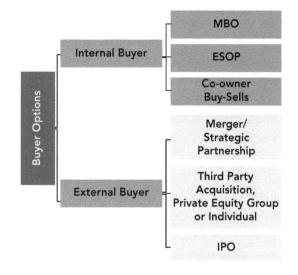

What are the trends in ownership transfer? There are four words for this: *it depends and in flux.*

It depends refers to whether you are a small business or mid-market company. Small business buyers tend to buy a *job* or income stream, whereas middle market buyers are typically *investors* evaluating the risk associated with an expectation of long-term returns.

In flux means there has been a shift in owner preferences and the dynamics of intergenerational family businesses. A recent survey of small business owners reported that about one-third of affluent owners plans to sell to a third party. Another one-third plan to sell to family members, about 18 percent plan to sell to employees and about 16 percent plan to close their doors. These trends have changed in the last few years.[46]

For family-owned firms, it was once a sacred principle, and the default option, that ownership transferred within the family. In the late '90s, fewer than five percent of family-owned companies wanted to sell to outsiders.[47] By 2010, in family-owned small businesses, 47 percent considered selling to an external company or investor.[48]

Here is a basic illustration of the ownership transfer options. It begins with the question, "Is your buyer a potential internal successor or an external person or entity?"

Internal Buyer Options

MBO: A Management Buyout is a general category of sales where a single key employee, a group or all employees assume ownership. Lenders tend to be more interested in financing an MBO than an external buyer if internal buyers can demonstrate their ability to carry on with the business. Within this category are:

- **ESOP/Ts:** An Employee Stock Option Program/Trust is a buyout strategy where a company establishes a trust (ESOT) into which company stock or cash is contributed. These are allocated to employees for the eventual buyout of the original owners or for other purposes such as raising working capital or charitable giving, for example. Technically, an ESOP is a tax-qualified defined contribution benefits plan. As such, the funds are tax deductible by the corporation. S corporation stock owned by an ESOP is not subject to federal tax. Funding an ESOP is a long-term exit strategy and requires a decision to eliminate other buyer options. Find an ESOP specialist to determine if this is a viable option for your business.

- **Co-owner Buy-Sell Arrangement:** This arrangement provides for a shareholder or partner buyout of an exiting partner(s) or shareholders. It has advantages over an external buyer in that there is no need for a broker, but an attorney is essential, and payment terms are usually defined in operating, shareholder or partner agreements. Financing, however, can be difficult if large amounts of capital are needed or if there is little lead-time for co-owners to line up the funds.

This was our firm's preferred strategy. It required discipline and commitment to capture the funds quarter by quarter to finance the buyout. It also proved the rubric, "There is no such thing as new money." In our case, the pool of funds for the buyout included, in part, some of the dollars that would normally have been in the year-end partner profit distribution over the buyout horizon. As an owner, in the end, I traded their money over a short period for the money I would have earned over a four to five year post-exit period. They realized all the gains in the future growth as their ROI. I no longer had to put in the hours, energy and airline miles for mine.

External or Third Party Buyer Options

Private Equity Group (PEG) and Leverage Buyout (LBO) A Leveraged Buyout (LBO) is where a buyer (often an investment firm) buys a controlling interest in a business using a small amount of equity or cash and a large amount of external debt financing. This option re-emerged in the early years of this century with record purchases of private companies and divisions of larger corporations. Private Equity Groups (PEG) raise investment capital in funds subscribed to by "limited partners," i.e., individuals, endowments, institutional investors, etc. As new owners, PEGs may install new management and place performance targets on the acquired firm. Another variation of the PEG buyout is a "Sponsored Buyout" where a PEG buys out the founder (or infuses growth capital) and takes an ownership interest along with existing management.

Here are two considerations in selecting a buyout or investment by a PEG. *If* you have solid performance and strong management that is recognized by the PEG, it can be a good partner for growth; it brings a depth of financial savvy and industry knowledge. It wants to see the business succeed. However, a PEG is an investment fund with fixed lifetimes (its own exit strategy). For example, a PEG may set a limit of the first five years as the investment phase and five more years to realize the desired return on the invested capital to the partners. In other words, the goal is always to improve bottom line performance and liquidate the fund, i.e., your company. Thus, company performance, in the short term, is everything. Pressure on management to achieve cost efficiencies, revenue growth and profit while servicing debt can be intense. If you are retained as the operating manager of your company after a PEG becomes an owner, be prepared for greater oversight and tough performance goals for you and/or your people.

Initial Public Offering or IPO An Initial Public Offering is the original sale of stock to the public as a means of transferring ownership, financing expansion or "cashing out." While often the strategy of young, emerging companies, it is also used by mid and large, privately owned companies. One advantage of an IPO is that it is a major liquidity event to the owner(s). It is their reward for growing a valued business. The seller is never required to repay the capital to its public investors and the capital raised for growth can be substantial. A disadvantage of an IPO strategy is the increase in federal and SEC regulations, greater legal exposure as an officer responsible for the misdeeds of the company and significant time required of officers to communicate with financial and fund analysts on financial and other information relevant to share value. You also incur costs associated with the IPO process: the investment in time and underwriters (usually investment bankers) to prepare a prospectus and the disclosure of private business information, which is now available to competitors, employees and vendors.

Finally, you must prepare your people for an IPO. There may be excitement about the benefits, but you must help them anticipate what will change. For example, communications practices that used to make people feel *in the know* will now be considered *insider information* and so cannot be shared spontaneously but disclosed according to SEC regulations. Also, consider if you are prepared for the changes in your privacy and personal life as with the disclosure of your financial compensation and the added obligation of bicoastal road shows and analysts calls.

Strategic Alliance/Joint Venture A *Strategic Alliance* or strategic partnership is an agreement between two or more companies to pursue an initiative collaboratively while remaining independent organizations. You and your strategic partner each contribute resources, such as intellectual property, funding, distribution channels, manufacturing or logistics capability and specialized knowledge to create a synergy not possible otherwise as individual entities. It is intended to mitigate risk through those synergies.

Strategic alliances have great appeal because they allow each party to concentrate on the activities that best fit their capabilities, promote knowledge transfer and share risk and reward. The failure rate of strategic alliances, however, is over 60 percent. A key factor in their success is how well you attend to the startup process that sets out operating principles and builds trust.

A *Joint Venture* (JV) is a business agreement where parties agree to work together to achieve a significant business objective of mutual importance by establishing, for a finite time, a new entity with contributed assets and equity. They exercise joint control over the enterprise and consequently share revenues, expenses and assets. Well known strategic alliances are Starbucks and Barnes and Noble to create in-store coffee houses; or Cisco and Xerox, where Xerox is imparting printer intelligence into Cisco technologies at the same time Cisco technologies is influencing Xerox's suite of cloud-based products.

Strategic Alliances and JVs are often testing grounds for the *fit* of two companies prior to an acquisition or merger although this is not always articulated up front.

Acquisition: Individual or Outside Company Acquisition here means the sale of your business to an external third party, either another company or an individual. Sometimes an acquisition is labeled a merger as when two companies of equal strength become one. It is seldom true in practice. As a client stated, "There is always, in fact, a *chomper* and the *chompee.*"

A groundbreaking study of mergers and acquisitions several years ago estimated that 83 percent of mergers and acquisitions failed to produce shareholder gains and in 50 percent of the cases studied actually destroyed value. This sale option, even for small businesses, is challenging, requiring the most due diligence and leadership of the several transfer choices. Those that succeed in preparing in advance have healthy balance sheets, use post-close transition agreements and utilize a broker or other merger and acquisition expert.

Your Options at a Glance

The chart on the next two pages compares the five basic exit options on six areas. It illustrates, for example, how an owner's philosophy may differ if he sells to a third party versus insiders; what the key management tasks are for each strategy; some of the advantages and disadvantages of each option and the typical time horizon involved. This chart doesn't exhaust the differences in options but allows you to explore and assess possible options with your advisor.

	Close & Liquidate	Sell to Insiders	Sell to 3rd Party (Acquisition)	Strategic Alliance (to an equal or larger firm)	Merger
Owner Philosophy	• It was a great ride and wealth creation; its time is over. • Realize final asset value now.	• Create a legacy firm on with ROE pay out by business. • Develop key employees or partners over time	• Fix up business to sell; cash out at sale; leave mgmt to new buyer. • Sponsored Buy-out by a Private Equity group.	• Collaborate but remain independent. Each contribute unique abilities and resources. Intent often to merge.	• A long term growth strategy with a planned owner exit and acceptance of loss of power.
Key Mgmt Tasks	• Correctly define and value assets: including intangibles. • Provide for soft landing for people	• Develop shared visions & strategy; • Recruit +/or develop successors • Transfer client relationships • Implement sustainable processes	• Financial documentation • Operating efficiencies • Strong successors and employment agreements • Legal and regulatory "purity"	• Prove out compatibility w. new "partner" • Protect value for exit; protect clients should partnership fail	• As in acquisition plus post close: culture assimilation • Integration of key functions. • Key talent retention • Power allocation
Valuation approach* & Key Costs Vet with your CPA	• Asset value = market price of items. • Distribution of "net" to owners by equity % (tax issues) • Employee severance, early lease buy-outs etc.	• "It's YOUR money buying you out." • LOW valuation to avoid double taxation "$1.82 rule"	• "It's their money buying you out." • HIGH and credible valuation desirable • External valuation costs	• Valuation occurs post alliance at the time of 'buy out' • Negotiated "price" from proving results	• As in an acquisition plus agreement by boards on equivalencies of value between co's.

	Column 1	Column 2	Column 3	Column 4	Column 5
Advantages	• Quickest option • Transaction approach • Cash out or perhaps cash plus % of future proceeds /royalties from data base.	• Measure of control during buy out • Continuity of culture/mission • Client relationships strengthened	• Cash at close • New Mgmt has experience • Clear set of time limited tasks on familiar "technical work".	• Partnership of "equals" – proven track records • "Prove out" time provides transition for both orgn's; i.e. less disruption.	• Potentially 'deep pockets' to finance the merger; Compensation and rewards may be enhanced
Disadvantages	• May be few actual assets to sell; difficult to define intangible asset value; • People lose their jobs • Those who regret it had no other option	• Employees don't have cash! • Partner time investment high and long horizon • Longer the runway = greater $ risk • Not all key employees = owner material.	• At mercy of financial markets and economy – FMV • "So long Charlie" – little transition • Hard feelings by emp. possible • Company will change.	• Risk that it becomes a 'force out' • Power is seldom equally divided • Defining measures of growth, success, difficult.	• Integration issues are resource intense • Long term cash out horizon required; high tolerance for risk • Low control over performance and results
Time Horizon	• 3-9 months	• 2-4 years – the sooner you start the better.	• 1-3 yrs – depending on condition of company & markets	• 1-3 yrs – rare that it isn't really an acquisition.	• 1-4 years – unpredictable tenure post close.

The Reality of the Buyer Pool

My grandson is madly in love with Ford Mustangs, especially vintage ones. At car shows, you can see his knees go weak as he nears one. We even text him pictures if we see an especially cool (or hot) Mustang. His mother, of course, wants him to drive a practical, i.e., safe and recent model SUV. Such is the heartache of love and reality.

Like a teenager and Chevalier's man in love, fantasy and hopes can cloud your decision process about the right girl, a.k.a. buyer. In searching for who best should take over your business, you can lose touch with reality. You may see the deep pockets of a potential buyer, but not whether they are a strategic fit or what their values and goals are regarding your company. You may admire the entrepreneurial spirit and drive of a Millennial buyer but fail to fully explore their financial ability to really purchase the business. Shedding light on the process saves you time and frustration. Know your buyer profile criteria is a key step in that process.

To shed light on the process, begin with knowing the two basic kinds of buyers and their goals.

- *Strategic Buyers* are operating companies that provide products or services and are often competitors, suppliers or customers of your firm. They can also be unrelated to your company, but looking to grow in your market to diversify their revenue sources. Their goal is to identify companies whose products or services can synergistically integrate with their existing P&L to create incremental long-term shareholder value. The defining word is "synergy."
- *Financial Buyers* include private equity groups, also known as financial sponsors, hedge funds, family investment offices and ultra-high net worth individuals. These firms and executives are in the business of making investments in companies and realizing a return on their investments (ROI). Their goal is to identify private companies with attractive future growth opportunities and competitive advantages in which to invest capital and realize a healthy return from a sale or an IPO. The defining words are ROI and growth.

Because these buyers' objectives differ, the lens they use in their due diligence is different. While both groups will judiciously evaluate a business, *strategic buyers look for the likelihood of integration and synergy* while financial buyers target *potential earnings growth and cash-generating capability.* Which is the better fit for your company and your hopes for its continuation after you leave?

There are also two emerging sub-categories of buyer with unique agendas from the strategic or financial buyer. These are:

• Late Bloomer Buyers
• Ready-to-Wear Buyers

A business owner was compiling a list of potential buyers for his business. Last on his list of prospective buyers was, "Someone who wants to buy their own job." In fact, recent research shows that more individuals are choosing a post-retirement career jump to business ownership. In a survey of thousands of business buyers, sellers and agents across Canada, the U.S., U.K., Australia and South Africa, it was found that 20 percent of today's buyers were over 55 (the *Late Bloomer* buyer) and another 30 percent were between 44 and 55 (The *Ready-to-Wear* buyer). The top reasons cited for buying a business included: 1) the independence of owning their own business, 2) the desire to expand or move into a new area of business and 3) the dream of escaping the rat race.

The share of new business owners between 50 and 65 is up almost 10 percent since 1996. Boomers, as innovative as younger generations, are seeking outlets for their energy and ideas through business ownership. They are more educated, have higher incomes, more disposable wealth, substantial work experience and are willing to take risks. *Late Bloomer buyers* bring all of this to the management of a business.[53]

The *Ready-to-Wear* buyer is looking for the job called CEO of a well-run business. They can see the upside in the technology or market as well as where new leadership (and an infusion of capital) can provide the opportunity to run and grow something of their own without having to launch a start-up. It's not far-fetched to consider these individuals are looking to buy their own job as prospective buyers.

You need to understand the different buyer categories for another reason; the due diligence on these buyers will be slightly different. Because you value sustainability and legacy in your exit planning, you must pay attention to factors that affect your people and customers.

For strategic buyers, in addition to their financial qualifications, you want to know about the corporate culture, top management team and the post-purchase transition/integration plan. For financial buyers, you examine their operational style and the track record of managing and holding a company. With Late Bloomer buyers and Ready-to-Wear buyers, you want to shed enough light on their experience and goals to know if what you are selling is a decent fit and what repairs or alterations they might expect in order to give you a full price offer.

Your Profile Criteria

Here's a final note on buyer categories. Men and women differ when they think about to whom they might sell. Women owners who plan to sell are more concerned than their men counterparts about:

- The buyer's identity, personality and background (72% versus 39%)
- The buyer's plans for the business (79% versus 52%)
- The buyer's plans for current employees (86% versus 61%)

Be sure these three factors are in your buyer profile. They account for a significant proportion of post-sale regrets by sellers who value leaving a sustainable company.

By taking the time to write out your buyer criteria in advance, you are prepared should an unexpected offer or inquiry come in. It's similar to knowing your car buying criteria, which stops you from hastily buying the flashy Mustang with a for-sale sign in the rear window.

There's no sense advertising a two-seater sports car to a population looking for a minivan. Knowing the profile of the right buyer and characteristics of the buyer pool makes your selling process more *efficient*. You spend less time with unqualified buyers and suffer less deal fatigue from false starts, false leads and dead ends.

ASK YOURSELF

- What do your legal agreements say about who may buy and how the decision to sell occurs?

- What is your image of the right buyer/owner for your company?
  – What vision and philosophy of management will be a fit with your company?

- If external buyers: Are they strategic or financial buyers? What are their value drivers, their deal breakers, their track record in acquisitions?

- If internal or family buyers: What do you know about their career objectives, growth potential, vision for the business and their deal breakers?

- What are your *red flags*, e.g., financing, competition, customer or supplier issues, personal reputation/characteristics, values or behaviors?

- What do you know about the current buyer pool for your business, for example, age groups, net worth and motivations? What is the size and forecast for it over the next two years, e.g., grow, shrink, be tougher or more flexible? What financing options do they have as buyers given capital markets?

In Conclusion

Here in Step 5, you focused on calculating the value of your business, defining your preferred transfer process and creating your desired buyer profile. This work is both analytical and emotional. There is little room for error in these areas so working with a team of technical advisors is essential.

PUT THE RUBBER ON THE ROAD – VALUATION AND BUYERS

The right valuation methodology depends on your operating agreements, your financial goals and your business type. Use a qualified valuation expert and be prepared to modify your thinking.

Your basic revenue options are: an outright sale, a phased sale or dissolution. Each has options within them from cash to seller to LBOs to owner financing and others. Know how they differ and affect your financial, estate and tax planning.

You have choices in defining your buyer options ranging from MBO to ESOP to third party acquisition and a co-owner buyout. Buyers have their own diverse objectives, e.g., strategic or financial. Know the profile of your desired buyer so you can better position your company.

SCENIC OVERLOOK

REVENUE OPTIONS AND YOUR BUYER PROFILE

Now you start to close in on your options for how you will sell your business and to whom. Here are three worksheets: one on transfer options and two to explore your thinking on the buyer profile.

This work is so critical and will require outside expertise to do the analysis that considers your goals, your financial strength, the company value and the market for your business. These worksheets help you begin your thinking and personal analysis to determine what you know vs. what you need to learn.

I. EXPLORING YOUR TRANSFER OPTIONS

Use the following worksheet to explore your thinking about your transfer options. What questions does this raise for you? With whom do you need to discuss them?

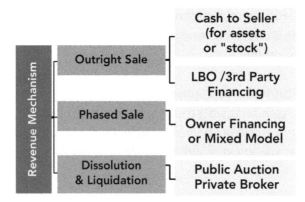

1. What is your ideal regarding your cash out: Outright sale? Gradual or phased buyout? Interim co-ownership or liquidation? Other?	
2. What are the pros and cons of each given your circumstances and long-range goals?	
3. What do you know about buyers' preferences in today's economy?	
4. What information, if anything, do you need?	
5. How can your advisors help you in deciding your best options?	

II. THE IDEAL BUYER

A. *Construct Your List*

First, you must determine what your preference is for where a buyer comes from, inside or outside your company / family.

Second, by what mechanism do you prefer that the ownership be transferred?

Finally, when you envision the new owner, what do you picture in terms of these criteria?

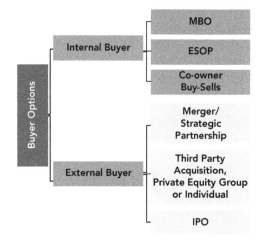

1. Strategic versus Financial buyer? Late Bloomer? Ready-to-Wear?	
2. Experience and background	
3. Fit with your company: vision, personality, management philosophy	
4. Financial profile	
5. Role in the company (active versus passive)	
6. View on customer and supplier relationships	
7. Track record of acquisitions and transitions, if a third party buyer	

B. Simplify Your Decision Criteria for Who Should Buy

Here are six high-level factors that owners seem to anguish over when thinking about their exit strategy. Each factor is on a continuum with two poles to distinguish the choice to be made.

For example, is your number one goal in selling the business to get the highest return on your investment/equity, namely, a big profit? Is it to leave a legacy and a sustainable business that endures beyond your ownership? This is not to say you don't care about both, but you must be very clear on your first priority.

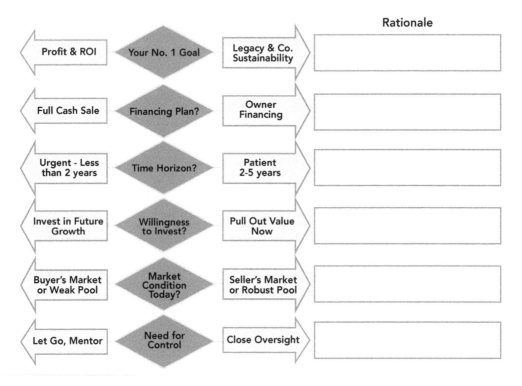

Directions: Think about each factor and place an X where you think you fall on its continuum. Beware! Marking your answers down the middle does not serve to bring clarity. Push your thinking to declare a preference. Make a note for each on your rationale. Summarize what your choices seem to say about what is important to you and what is suggested about your transfer options.

STEP 6 ~ SECURE YOUR COMPANY'S SUSTAINABILITY

The purpose of business is to create and keep a customer.

Peter Drucker

Sustainability has a simple definition – the staying power of the culture, people, systems and processes that safeguard your company's value after you leave. In Step 6, you focus on the *processes and practices* that sustain value. These are mature business processes that enable low operating costs; and practices that sustain customer loyalty and their revenue stream, and which retain key talent during and after the selling process.

MATURE YOUR BUSINESS PROCESSES

Do you remember learning how to drive a car? That learning process is analogous to how your company may have created its business processes. They both started out simply, a bit ad hoc, complete with stalls, uneven operation and, happily, forward motion. Sometimes there was shouting about what was right or wrong and at other times wonderment when there weren't more accidents or defects! The learning process evolved over time, although not always for the better.

You probably don't own a business because you love the back office transactions or alphabet soup of processes (MRP, ERP and CRM). Process management simply isn't that exciting. Just like learning to drive, once the license was awarded, attending to the driving process was forgotten—until that first traffic ticket. The same is true with business processes. Once you win that contract, deliver the product or see an invoice paid, there is little looking back to see what the true cost of those efforts were and how they could be improved.

As your business becomes more complex with multiple products, more people, larger customer base, and more functions, several things happen. Often duplicate legacy systems are built to fit the unique needs of a business unit or individual manager. Second processes tend to reside in the creator's head versus publicly documented so others can manage them. This works until suddenly it doesn't. When the process creators leave, they take with them the *how it really works* knowledge. As technology and customer requirements change, responding to them requires massive re-engineering costs while legacy system owners resist the changes.

The graphic here is based on the model by the Engineering Institute at Carnegie Mellon University.[55] Simply, the stages of process maturity depend on the cost, consistency, and capability of a process to meet or exceed customer requirements.
The lower your processes are on this maturity curve, the more they are unreliable, costly, and a barrier to growth.

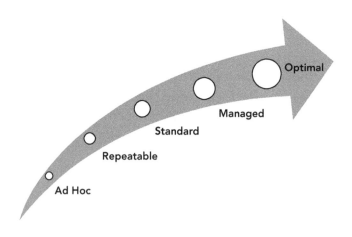

This framework can be used to evaluate and identify processes in your business that need improvement plans. Where your processes truly rank on maturity levels requires more than hunches. Methodologies rich in measurement and root cause analysis, such as LEAN or LEAN-Six Sigma, are needed to provide the most accurate assessment. What you want to know is a) how is a process performing against customer needs and at what cost to your business? and b) are these processes a threat to your business value and sustainability?

Look for an Opportunity to Mature

Here is an example of what asking performance questions can reveal about very simple business activity.

When our firm was about to have its first million dollar revenue year, our office manager was frustrated that so many of our invoices were considerably exceeding our 30-day receivables target. As a professional services company, accounts receivables and payroll/payables were the main factors in our operating cash flow and ability to invest in our growth.

Our office manager asked the partners a simple question, "What do you do after you win a contract to set up how we get paid?" We each drew our own process map. Not surprising, we all had different practices. More importantly, however, as individuals, we didn't always do the same thing the same way every time. In other words, we had an ad hoc process.

So she collected data on late payments and did a Pareto analysis to describe the characteristics of the aging problem. When we looked at the data, the root cause and the solution were obvious and simple: we needed to create a standardized payment process based on the client requirements and our business imperative. We needed to control it by following a checklist and manage it by consistently evaluating its performance.

In a couple of brief meetings, we took an "Ad hoc" process that felt mindless to the partners and moved it all the way up the maturity scale to "Managed." This simple change reduced the number of non-conforming receivables by nearly 90 percent within four months. More important, our cash flow and conversion cycle improved, and our Office Manager was more productive not having to chase down late payments.

Your cash conversion cycle is of great interest to a buyer. It signals how well your processes, e.g., project fulfillment, billing and supplier payables, are operated and managed. It's a clue as well to your liquidity strength. Efficient, effective processes make a business scalable and independent of an owner. These attributes are keys to salability and sustainability.

These days, a process-focused buyer can look at budgets and financials to see the underlying processes at work. You must also understand what processes drive the value of your business and make sure your company story highlights the level of maturity you have achieved.

Bridge Actions:

Use the tools in this chapter's Scenic Overlook to examine your core processes and identify where an improvement bridge plan is needed for core processes. Meanwhile, ask yourself:

- How much alignment is there on the top five business processes that drive revenues, profitability, customer satisfaction, and your people's productivity?
- Ask those who work *in* one of those key processes, e.g., invoicing or project budget tracking, and those who *receive* the output of those processes, customers, partners, internal operations, how the process is working. What is their accuracy, timeliness, cost or the rework required?
- What's your *hunch* about the maturity level of your key processes and what performance data would validate your hunch?
- Where is your biggest process exposure, i.e., where process costs would show up in buyer due diligence? Where is an improvement plan needed?

SECURE CUSTOMERS AND REVENUE STREAMS

Customers and revenue streams are vulnerable when a company is on the market. Your goal is to preserve the value of your revenue stream by focusing on the customer and anticipating their experience and reaction to a change in ownership. You must put in place a process for customer retention and revenue stability even before a prospective buyer is identified.

In small to mid-size companies, customer connections will influence and be influenced by a transfer of ownership. The effect of the sale of a private, closely held company on customer retention is hard to know, as statistics are not normally made public. The data are clear, however, for publicly traded companies. "Customer defections are a major reason why more than half of all mergers fail to deliver the intended improvement in shareholder value…".[56] Too often, companies focus post-close, on the internal goals of consolidation and integration at the expense of the customer who feels adrift and open to competitor enticements.

Anticipate Customer Reaction

To the small and mid-size business owner, *markets* don't write checks, customers do. Your share of the customer's wallet is the result of loyalty based on a relationship made up of many decisions made year after year about their experience, and your perceived value and trustworthiness. When you sell your business, that relationship is tested.

How do customers react when a valued supplier changes ownership, especially in an external acquisition? There are three predictable reactions: acceptance, concern and rejection. There are four factors influencing which reaction your customers will have.[57]

- How *close and trusted the relationship* is with the existing owner or the company, e.g., bonds established over the years via shared experiences. An additional consideration is how *linked* reputations and achievements are, such as prime/sub-prime contractor relationships.
- The *relationship of the customer to the prospective buyer*(s), e.g., previous negative experiences as a customer or a competitor of the new owner; concern for a change in the business relationships as a result of the sale, such as with sole source agreements or required non-compete agreements.
- The amount of *mutual and accurate information* about your and the buyer's intentions and the customer's assumptions about potential changes including costs or benefits to them from the sale.
- *Turbulence* in the operational aspects of the company post-close that negatively affect the customer's business such as changes in logistics, billing/payment or contracting processes.

We know that 20 percent of customers defect because of a poorly executed transition or integration.[59] If this happened to your business during the sale process or soon after, what would be the effect on your business and the terms of the sale, e.g., escrow or earn-out payments? Building a bridge plan to protect your relationship begins with a customer inventory, including the knowledge you have and don't have about them.

Inventory your Key Customers
Spend time gathering the following knowledge:

- What you know *factually* about the most important customers in your portfolio, those who drive 80 percent of your revenues and your reputation in your industry. For example, do you know their size of your revenue pie, contract expiration dates, or your vulnerability to competitors taking your place?
- What you know *personally* about those customers as a fellow business owner, such as "what keeps them awake at night;" what their values and goals are and what support they will need to make the transition to a new owner.

The template example below can be used to anticipate and plan retention activities between seller and buyer for the period before and following the close. For your top customers, how would you characterize their experience with you/your company? What is their experience with your potential buyer? What is the information they have about your goals, the sale, and a potential buyer and what is their understanding of it (e.g., assumptions they are making)? What turbulence might they experience from a change in owners?

With this information in hand, you can now assess what the implications are for you, your company and post-sale integration agreements with your buyer. Further, you will be better able to determine what communication plan will best support your customer.

Customer	Experience with Us	Experience with Buyer	Shared Information re: rationale-intention	Turbulence anticipated
"Big Inc."				
Implications: • Relationship management • Communication planning				

Bridge Actions:

1. **A Customer Transition Plan:** A transition plan should be established *prior* to your close. I suggest creating a transition team made up of both seller and buyer staff with a great deal of company and customer Knowledge. Their mission is to build and implement a customer retention plan that reduces customer concerns, prevents disruptions and maintains the relationship over the course of the transition from letter of intent to one year after the sale.

   Remember, your goal is to sustain the value of your company. You do this by creating the least turbulence and delivering the most unified experience for the customer ensuring their retention and goodwill.

2. **Communication and Personal Handoffs:** Expect a large debate among brokers and advisors about communication with customers prior to the close of your sale, especially in commodity-type businesses, professional services and medical practices. The argument goes like this:

   Customers are change averse. They buy "you" not just the service/product because they know you and don't know (or maybe they do and don't like) the new owner. They may hate the deal. Tell them as late as possible. Don't give time for competitors to use the sale against you with your customers.

   The argument certainly raises good cautions, but look at the underlying assumptions of this position:

   - You are out of touch with your customers and have to guess at their reaction or don't have a relationship with them that is open enough to allow proactive conversation, which would allow them to express and work through concerns or resistance.
   - That being for sale or going to retire isn't going to become known before you make it official anyway, which leaves you reacting to comments like, "How come I had to hear this from…?"
   - A transition and communications plan can't mitigate negative reactions, even though the research clearly points otherwise.

My bias is to plan a communications strategy based on your knowledge of your customers and that is face-to-face, President-to-President or your sales account manager and their contracts counterpart.

You know how to do this because doing business is personal to you; it's based on strong values for the integrity of the relationship. In my firm, this meant all exiting owner's major clients had a "second face to the customer" for at least a year before a partner exited the business. At client events, mingling time meant having joined-at-the-hip conversations with a client even if it was a 13-hour plane trip to be there. At the senior levels of our client organizations, we had explicit conversations foreshadowing the change in leadership to ensure we knew what they needed for a smooth transition. In a professional services company, this is essential. In a mid-size product company, the account executive needs to be empowered to speak to the valued relationship and bring in the exiting founder/owner when needed. This is a high-touch moment in your leadership.

3. **Due Diligence on buyer customer practices:** Number one, disregard assurances from a buyer that customers will not be affected. Second, research the buyer's reputation with customers including back office customers support. What are the strong and weak points of the current customer service that will likely carry on with the acquisition of your company? What is their customer problem-resolution process? What is the average life of a customer, i.e., churn? Finally, if the buyer has made any other acquisitions, what happened to administrative systems and/or customer field support in the first year?

In summary, planning for customer and revenue continuity means having the ability to confidently answer a few key questions:

ASK YOURSELF

- If you sold your business today and handed it to a new owner or partner to care for your customers, what would your customers experience? What would they notice from billing to service to their relationship with company officers or account managers? What would happen to their trust and confidence in the relationship?
- If this is a moderate to large merger or acquisition, does having a post-close transition team from both companies make sense? What are the transition priorities, e.g., transfer of customer knowledge, integration of CRM systems, personal visits?

RETAIN KEY TALENT

Your key talent is also vulnerable in an ownership transfer. Their vision of the future becomes cloudy; their sense of control is shaky. It costs money to replace and retrain people, but it's a different level of cost when it's a critical employee you want to keep to protect your company value and sustainability.

The kneejerk reaction to retention planning is a one-size-fits-all "golden handcuffs" plan. This will work with a minority of critical-to-keep people. What works better is knowing what the key talent on your must-keep list cares about, then taking a tailored, integrated approach to stay-incentives.

Who Are at Risk and What Do They Care About?

Not everyone in your company falls into the must-keep category, and not all of them are at risk of leaving. In addition, not all the critical-to-keep are your high potential people. Some are those with the institutional knowledge. Some are your thought leaders who, if they left, would send a signal to others to do the same. A few keepers in the short term are people who keep the business running smoothly, yet are replaceable if given time to train a replacement. Who are the people in these categories, what do they care about and what range of plans will support (you can't guarantee) their retention?

Companies that have talent management and reward programs as part of their ongoing people practices are a third less likely to lose *critical skill* employees and 18 percent less likely to lose *top-performing* employees."[59] These companies know what their key talent cares about and needs to remain motivated and committed. Then they match their retention plans to the unique employee risk profile. If you don't have this knowledge, you have but two options: guess or ask directly.

It's not all about money; non-financial motivations play a role. There are five factors people rate as the most effective motivators and satisfiers in their work: challenging, stimulating work; responsibility and opportunity for advancement; a sense of personal achievement and growth; salaries/wages/benefits that provide for security and lifestyle; and interpersonal relationships with boss and peers.

It's important to know what each key employee cares about in this time of uncertainty. Is it family disruption if relocation is required (security and lifestyle), or how this change may reflect on their resume (broader responsibility or growth)? The retention package for such diverse needs requires open discussions and creative approaches beyond the standard stay bonus.

What Makes a Retention Plan Work?

There are two ways to think about employee retention. First, how do you keep the people the business doesn't want to lose regardless of the timeframe? Second, how do you retain people you need for a specified period, such as until the close or through a specific transition period? These are two very different goals, and your retention plans must fit each goal. Your ultimate goal is to keep key players who are critical to your business and who might leave on <u>their</u> timing not yours.

Two common approaches are used to keep key talent during a sale. Stay-on bonuses pay for transitional services. Their duration can be short or phased, for example, staying through the closing (sometimes called Change of Control Bonus) or for a transition period with performance incentives. The second approach is an enhanced severance package tied to a point in time.

If you don't have a good talent management program in place, then accept that retention of key people will likely be costly, especially for the first category of key talent. They have the leverage. In fact, what most owners do is often not very successful. They offer stay bonuses to keep these people until a certain date, such as the close, and, predictably, the people then leave. Stay-on bonuses do not build trust nor does key talent perceive the value. Still, enhanced severance does give people income security in case the new owner terminates them and gives the departing owner and the buyer time to show that the business will be a good place to work.

For others whose jobs will be eliminated due to consolidation, a stay-on bonus with severance tied to key deliverables and dates can be effective. The best retention plans are a combination of stay-bonus and severance. These are specific to the individuals, the retention goal and a cost/risk analysis. The Scenic Overlook provides you with a tool to complete a specific analysis of your talent at risk to determine what retention approach makes sense.

Bridge Action:
1. Complete a retention risk assessment for key positions and people. Then gather up-to-date knowledge of target employees' motivations and concerns.

2. Define your budget and list of retention options – financial and non-financial. Then develop an overall retention plan based on the above.

3. Define individual offers and hold face-to-face meetings on the company's intentions and hopes for the target employee.

 ASK YOURSELF

- Do you have alignment on who are the critical-to-keep employees and what they care about?
- Have you defined a flexible approach to retention versus a one-size-fits-all plan?
- How can you use your retention plan to demonstrate sustainable value to prospective buyers?

IDENTIFY YOUR PERSONAL SUSTAINABILITY PATH: WHAT'S YOUR ROLE "AFTER?"

If you're like many owners, you wonder if you should have a continuing role in your business after you sell, especially if you are part of a family-run business or selling to an internal buyer. Considerations are where continuity is needed, where you can make a difference, and, what will the new owners want from you? These are *business* questions.

Then there are the questions about *motivational* needs: what role will be fulfilling and why? What are your needs for power, recognition, autonomy, achievement and/ or inclusion? Seldom are these needs explicitly discussed. It's your obligation to sort these out and define the right role for you. There isn't always a match, however, between what you or the new owners need.

Typically, post-departure roles last one year. In the most successful situations, your role is defined in writing and reviewed during the duration of the agreement. This applies to family-owned businesses as well.

Five Typical Roles

The five roles I typically see post-departure are:

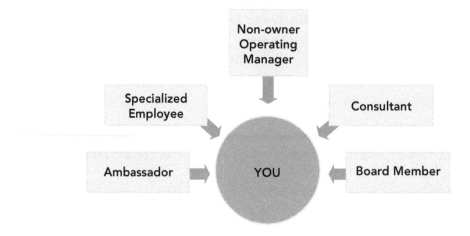

"Photo on the Wall" – Ambassador

Maybe for a founder, the best role is an ambassador whose photo is on the wall. You represent the legacy, reputation and goodwill of your former company with customers, community or industry groups. Ambassador roles are attractive for the continued attachment they provide. It can satisfy your recognition, social and inclusion needs. It is a noble role with the potential to be enormously beneficial and rewarding. In one company, the elderly founder became head of the family foundation, which had a large presence in the community. Being an ambassador requires you to be fulfilled by engaging in symbolic acts, not by managing operational results. Even with positive intentions, ambassador roles can draw you back into acting *as if* you are in a strategy or advisory role or obstruct the handoff of key relationships with customers or suppliers.

"A Specialized Me" – Reduced Employee Role

Another valuable role is *specialized me*. You remain on the payroll as a focused expert in a reduced role for a defined period, for example, as a technology chief or account executive to a key client. This role meets your need to relinquish control, yet can satisfy your achievement and social (affiliation) needs. An impressive example of this working well was a retail store owner who sold her business on a Friday and came to work as a sales clerk and trainer on Monday. She loved her limited role, and her new boss retained the best salesperson who knew each customer by first name. In a second example, a Christmas store owner sold her business but remained responsible for the massive holiday displays customers looked forward to seeing each year. These are encouraging examples but aren't always typical.

A specialized role is especially difficult in family-owned businesses. Seldom does a son or daughter exercise leadership with confidence when a parent moves from boss to underling. I interviewed a small business owner who struggled with the changes his son and daughter-in-law were making in the family business. The second generation had not been active in the business and bought it "to keep it in the family." The backgrounds of the founders and their children could not have been more different, including how they defined the critical success factors of the operation. After a year, Dad gave his notice in order to preserve the relationship.

On the other hand, I interviewed a wonderful founder and son whose long-range planning, mutual trust and shared philosophy from years of working together in their sporting goods business made the specialized role a success. For the year following the transfer of ownership, Dad managed particular customers and suppliers and their contract renewals.

"Almost Still in Charge" – Non-owner Operating Manager

Sometimes a Private Equity Group or larger acquiring company retains you in a *non-owner operating manager* position, e.g., President or COO. The benefit is that they have complete control of finance and strategy, yet the continuity of your valued operational experience and leadership. You have reduced your financial risk while on a runway to retirement. This role can satisfy your need for achievement but will be difficult if you have a high need for autonomy and control.

Performance expectations are usually written into an employment agreement as well as decision roles, authorities and revenue or production goals among other things. The best example of this was a five-year patient partnership between a large aerospace company and its acquisition of a small, privately held, systems engineering firm. The parent kept the founders in their leadership roles exercising strategy, maintaining operational control and nurturing client relationships.

"Guru" – Consultant

A common role for a departing owner is as *consultant* for a specified period. In this role, you may have clear deliverables and responsibilities or operate under a loosely defined role of *on-call advisor* to senior management. It is gratifying to be acknowledged for your expertise, and this role allows you to meet your recognition and inclusion needs. Two successful examples are: 1) a former partner provided the knowledge transfer of the intellectual property he had created, but which had not been widely disseminated, and 2) An exiting father-owner mentored a newly hired sales manager on key customer issues and product pricing strategy. He was present in the stores, as needed, which afforded a gentle withdrawal.

This role, however, is not a good fit if you have high control or achievement needs. Consultants have little control over resource allocation or the execution of a plan.

You may think this role is a given. It sounds like, "Of course I will offer to stay on to help with ...." Don't be surprised when the new owners don't offer it or when your offer is declined.

"Governance" – Board Member

In a company acquisition or merger, you, as exiting CEO, may join the board of directors. This role may be as a minor shareholder in the company or as a paid external director. This is typical in larger family businesses. The benefits are that you provide the continuity of perspective in the governance of the company, and customers may feel a sense of confidence in the sustainability of the company. You meet your power and inclusion needs through governance and, to a lesser degree, any need for achievement needs. However, a seat on a board may frustrate you if you imagine you will control operations or strategy execution.

Board roles sometimes produce conflict when the new operating executives change strategic direction or when company performance falters. New owners may cast about attempting to assign blame asking if it resides with the old regime or the new one.

At this crossroads in your business life, the best advice is to have the role conversation early in transition planning and negotiate an explicit post-close role. It should address the following questions:

- Will you, the departing owner, have a role in the operation of the business and if so, what?
- What are the specific continuing duties or deliverables and for how long?
- If the relationship sours, what will be the process for exiting the role and with what financial consequences?

In Conclusion

Your objective in Step 6 was to ensure your company's value and health continues after you leave. That meant creating bridge plans for any area that threatened continuity. You examined core business processes for maturity, preserving customer loyalty and revenue streams, and securing talent retention. Finally you looked at YOU. What role makes sense post-close?

SECURE COMPANY SUSTAINABILITY

Examine your core business processes against cost, quality and customer requirements. Improve their maturity.

Protect your revenue stream by anticipating the impact of the sale on your customers. Make a plan.

Minimize key talent loss by tailoring retention plans to your risks AND what key employees care about.

Examine what role makes sense for you and your company post-close. Don't assume there is a role for you. Get it in writing.

SCENIC OVERLOOK

SUSTAINABILITY TOOLS

Your company is like a classic sedan that has been driven for many miles on many journeys. You know its idiosyncrasies, and it's comfortable! At this stage of your life and career, you don't need to tear it down and restore it to new. That doesn't mean you won't make the repairs or alterations necessary to ensure its full value.

This Overlook provides you with several worksheets for looking at your: Business Processes, Customer Retention Plan, Key Talent Risk-Assessment, your Role in post departure sustainability, and your overall Communications Strategy.

You may not complete all of these at this time. Understand what they focus upon so you can allocate the time to do this work in a timely way.

I. BUSINESS PROCESS MATURITY

Your goal is to understand how process performance is affecting the value of your company, its salability, operational costs and overall profits. You start by identifying the core business processes, how they are being measured and to what degree they are meeting customer (internal and external) requirements. Where are they on the maturity continuum? Where do they need to be? With a decent time horizon to your exit, there is the opportunity to launch LEAN or other data-driven process improvement programs.

1. *Intuition:* Discuss with your management the maturity level, as defined below, of the three to five key processes (or sub-processes) critical to your business. Where, at a minimum level, do they need to be on the curve to improve the business and its value to a potential buyer/operator?

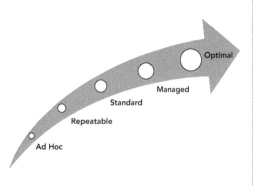

Optimal: Process is capable of meeting a SET of requirements (e.g. billing accuracy AND cost of transaction; drug testing process for efficacy AND safety AND margins AND insurance listing). It delivers the full value possible that is economically justifiable.

Managed: A Process Owner works to ensure the process meets effectiveness and efficiency goals; performance is known/tracked and continuously being improved.

Standard: Customer requirements and process measures are used to determine if the process is operating well and what its cost is to the business.

Repeatable: "As Is" Process is documented, and people follow this each time it is performed.

Ad Hoc: "Ad hoc," often chaotic and costly; performance reliability and quality are undocumented.

2. **Verify:** Ask those who work *on* one of those key processes or sub-processes (e.g., quarterly financial reports, hiring or billing) and those who *receive* the output of those processes (customers, partners, internal operations) the following:

    a. How well are the processes working? E.g., how much rework, waste or late delivery is there?

    b. What data do they have to track how the process is performing? What data would be helpful?

3. **Compare:** how do these answers match your estimates and with industry data if available. Chances are the farther away from the process you are, the bigger the gap in your knowledge.

4. **Implications:** What are the implications of what you learn for improving the value of the business?

II. CUSTOMER RETENTION ANALYSIS

Directions:

List the customers who drive approximately 80 percent of your revenue. Evaluate the factors that influence the relationship with each. Discuss these four areas:

1. What has been the experience of this customer with us, e.g., our shared knowledge and history, problem resolution process, professional and personal relationships (such as serving on industry boards together)?
2. What experience has our customer had with our potential buyer? Is a mitigation plan needed? If these are unknowns, what is the plan to find out the information?
3. How well does this customer understand our intention in transferring ownership? What is needed to ease concerns or build support?
4. What post-close transitions in our administrative systems might create disruption for this customer/client, e.g., technology, or people like sales account leaders?
5. How vulnerable are we to losing this customer to a competitor?

Customer	Experience with Us	Experience with Buyer	Shared Information e.g. Rationale	Turbulence Anticipated
•				
•				
•				
•				

Customer Transition Management Priorities and First Next Steps

1.

2.

III. KEY TALENT RETENTION

A. Analysis

Directions:

1. Identify the attributes important for retention. Those on the left column below are suggestions.

2. Determine YOUR color code for the matrix (degree of pain you will feel if this group was to leave) and which cells it covers. For example, e.g., Red = high risk and strategic, (immediate action required); Dark Green = high risk and key to stable operations during the transition (contingency plans needed); Pink = moderate risk and temporary pain – initiate planning.)

3. Place your key people into the matrix cells.

Difficulty to replace (Hard → Easy)		0	25	50	75	100
Hard	Unique technical or process knowledge critical to sustainability					
	Thought leader who influences a large following (internal or external)					
	Important knowledge/skill set; but there are internal substitutes given a bit of time.					
Easy	Valued competencies; if lost, create short-term pain					

Risk level the person will leave

B. Retention Strategies

1. Identify key talent motivators/concerns: Financial? Career? Family? Growth/challenge?

2. List your retention options: promotion, retention bonus, development/training, special assignment, new tools/technology investment, a new manager and workplace flexibility, to name a few.

3. Define your retention strategy. What *mix* of retention strategies (financial and non-financial) will work with these individuals? Remember, *one size does not fit all and money isn't always the solution.*

C. Action:

1. Who owns the plan?

2. What are the first next steps?

3. What is our timeline for assuring key talent retention?

4. When will we reconvene to discuss progress?

IV. BUILD AN OVERALL COMMUNICATIONS PLAN

Use the simple framework below to plan your communications with each of your stakeholder groups: family, customers or select groups of employees, as well as the appropriate timing. This is not a static *one-time plan* but subject to updates as the sales process continues. Plan your communication specific to each audience. The first row provides things to consider as you build your communications plan. You will use this again in Step 8.

Audience	Purpose and Timing?	Possible Message Elements
• Key Managers? • Customers? • Family?	• Inform? • Build Commitment? • Create dialogue? • Provide direction? • Cause action?	• Strategy or Vision as Rationale? • Buyer Profile for "best fit"? • Timelines? • Communication Process?
Audience	**Your Central Purpose and Timing**	**2 to 3 Main Points**
• • •	• • •	• • •

V. SUSTAINABILITY ROLES AND YOU

- What role does your company *under its new ownership* most need to be filled? What are the indications that this is an accurate assumption? Who would agree?

- What are your emotional needs or motivational drivers that must be met for a role to be fulfilling? (Think in terms of achievement, control, power, affiliation/inclusion, autonomy/independence and/or recognition.)

- What role might fulfill those motivations? Define a role if none of the above is a good fit.

- What might the contract or agreement with the new owner look like for such a role, with what deliverables, boundaries, timeframes or periodic evaluations?

STEP 7 ~ GEAR UP FOR THE SALE

Ladies and Gentlemen, start your engines!

Indianapolis 500 race tradition

Let's assume you have defined your exit objectives, determined the value and salability of your company and your desired buyer profile. You have assessed the readiness of your business and are in the process of giving it a tune-up. You feel ready to hang out that For Sale sign.

The sales process is a set of activities that can be stressful even with the best preparation. Without preparation, it can be a nightmare. One broker advisor stated that he had seen the selling process age a person ten years. There are basic actions you must take to prevent drama and manage the stress. These actions involve the drafting, reviewing and/or updating of legal documents.

ADJUST YOUR CALENDAR

Once Steps 1 through 6 are underway, and the for sale sign goes up, prepare to divert 30 to 60 percent of your time away from the day-to-day tasks of running your business to the business of selling it. Your time will be spent:

- Reviewing potential buyer profiles presented by your Broker and interviewing for information; or, if you don't have a broker actively promoting, networking and prospecting for buyers, then you will be qualifying them instead
- Preparing and making pitches to buyers
- Facilitating buyer due diligence on your business, responding to requests for information and conducting your due diligence on the buyers

- Negotiating and contracting including conferring with your advisors, holding meetings with buyers to finalize terms and conditions and closing requirements
- Communicating with employees, suppliers, customers and your family or board

Don't be surprised when the demand for your time accelerates the further you are into the exit and sale process. You will not only spend time on the selling tasks, but on *thinking* about them. If emotions begin to run high during the sales process, if turnaround time for information speeds up and meetings become more frequent, you can expect longer days and seven-day work weeks.

PROTECT YOUR INTERESTS IN THE SALES PROCESS

There is a set of legal documents to facilitate the sales process and prevent crises. These documents inform, prescribe and protect a business and its owners, as well as prospective buyers during the sales process.

a. Informational Documents:
   - Selling memo (aka the briefing on the company story)
   - Confidential information memorandum (a more formal and complete disclosure of the company picture)

b. Sales Process Agreements:
   - A confidentiality or non-disclosure agreement (NDA)
   - Letter of intent
   - Closing documents, e.g., purchase/sales agreement, settlement statement, escrow agreement

c. Entity documents: such as operating agreements and legal entity filings

Informational Documentation

Your Company Story or Simplified Selling Memo
The first of these sales documents is your Company Story also called the Selling Memo. Your company story creates a link between your hopes for a profitable exit and a buyer's hopes for a profitable ongoing concern. It needs to tell an honest and

optimistic story that gives a snapshot that appeals to a buyer's needs and objectives and encourages further interest. The story can be a high-level management presentation or something resembling a brochure.

There is a simple framework for organizing your story, anticipating the list of buyer questions and requests for data. The six categories below help buyers evaluate the fit of your company with their agenda, goals and their key value drivers. In addition to providing a basic business description, the company story includes:

Financial Strength: e.g., 3-5 years financials, internal/external audits, legal/contract history and tax records, compensation plans, benefits liabilities
Growth Potential: e.g., 3-5 yr pro formas or revenue projections, return on investment, market share, competitive positioning , customer contracts, sole source agreements
Synergies: e.g., core competencies , intellectual property, product pipelines, vertical integration, customer bases
People: e.g. management team and key technical talent, HR policies, practices and liabilities including employment agreements for key talent retention, etc.
Brief History: when founded and by whom, growth milestones, changes in ownership or leadership, legal entity status, any changes over time
Selling Objectives: why selling and goals, offering price, initial terms and conditions

A Confidential Information Memorandum

A Confidential Information Memorandum is your detailed sales brochure. It is given to a qualified prospective buyer *upon their signing a confidentiality agreement*. For small companies, it may be only nine or ten pages. For larger companies, it may be the size of a small book of over 50 pages. There are three caveats to observe in your memorandum: a) brevity wins the day, b) do not include proprietary trade secrets, competitive pricing details or customer proprietary information and c) an internal buyer should be as knowledgeable as an external buyer; don't assume they already know the full picture.

There is no standard requirement for what is included in a memorandum, but the following is typically included:

a. Business Description
- Products/services
- Customers/client profile (diversity and concentration)
- Markets and geographic distribution
- Competitive advantage and core competencies

b. Ownership
- Legal structure
- Shareholders and percentage ownership
- Relevant operating agreements

c. Performance - Historical, Current and Projections
- Financial highlights including,
    - Historic and adjusted EBITDA
    - Cash flow analyses
    - Average growth rates
    - Summary historical balance sheets supported by tax returns
- Market share and penetration and industry trends
- Sales trends, cost of sales and customer acquisition
- Projected income statement summary, projected EBITDA and forecasted growth

d. People and Organization
- Size of the employee population and breakdown
- Key technical talent and leadership bench strength
- Organization structure, span of control and key culture attributes

e. Strengths, Opportunities and Risks or Challenges
- Plans for capitalizing on opportunities and for mitigating risks/challenges

f. Why Are You Selling? Why Now?
• Business rationale
• Personal vision, if appropriate

g. Offering Price and Terms
• What is for sale? e.g., hard assets, customer lists, IP and fair market value
• Bases for pricing/valuation
• Financing requirements and offers
• Timeframe of the sale

Preparing the memorandum can reinforce the great work you've done on exit planning or expose your vulnerabilities before prospective buyers uncover them, such as where you need financial data, issues with bench strength or gaps in risk management plans.

The Terms and Conditions Sheet

The Terms and Conditions sheet defines the explicit requirements and stipulations of your sale. They are your starting position statement and are subject to negotiation, ranging from what is to be sold and at what price to with what restraints post-close. It is the basis for your sales agreement once there is consensus. The components are described below under sales process agreements.

BUILD A SUPPORTING DATA BANK AND DATA CREDIBILITY

You will need to assemble hard data, i.e., information that supports the story of historical and projected performance and sustainability. The valuation and salability of your business is a function of the credibility and completeness of your data, documentation and analytical methods. As noted in Step 4, selling success improves 60 to 70 percent when financial data is complete, accurate and verified, especially by tax returns and external audit reports. Collecting documents and analyzing and interpreting data can be a true sinkhole of time and resources. Let's try to simplify the work.

Think of documentation as falling into two major categories – performance documents and legal documents. These documents must be credible, i.e., accurate, in compliance with legal or industry standards, believable and aligned with each other where appropriate.

Performance documents include historical and current financial reports and data (balance sheets, income statements, and tax records to name a few). The characteristic of good performance data/records is credibility, which includes accuracy, compliance, completeness and believability.

Legal documents means contracts (e.g., customer, supplier, real estate and employee) as well as operating and shareholder agreements. The quality of this documentation rests on currency, compliance and alignment.

Accuracy: Accuracy comes from 1) completeness of data, 2) the validity and truthfulness of the measurement system used to produce it and 3) a belief that the analytics used to translate the data into information are the right ones. Making sure it has all three quality characteristics is a huge task. You're collecting it or reconstructing if it is missing, verifying or validating sometimes through outside expertise, even copying and preparing report binders or securing electronic document files. One owner told me he and his wife spent over 100 hours just collecting and copying 20 years of data stored in paper files, so they could begin to analyze and prepare the reports required for a buyer's due diligence. Another executive in a 100-person company said that incomplete historical information and documentation was their biggest headache and threatened to derail the presentation of a credible company performance story.

Compliance: You are *in compliance* when you can confirm that your processes, reports, products, intellectual property and contracts meet the requirements of prescribed laws, regulations and generally accepted standards and practices. Non-compliance has legal consequences, such as litigation or shut down and financial consequences, such as fines. It may reduce the value of your company, spoil a deal and add onerous terms and conditions to mitigate buyer risk. A review of your accounting systems and audit reports in accordance with relevant regulatory compliance and legal contracts will improve your credibility.

Believability: Validity of projections and forecasts rests on making your assumptions explicit. Buyers want to know the basis for your conjectures and estimates about the future performance of the company, the industry, your technology advantages and the contribution of key talent to the strategy. If the historical data is weak or, assumptions are wrong, the forecasts are, too. Using an external validation of assumptions, such as benchmark data, industry statistics and economic indicators improve believability. Using a reputable advisor or broker does as well.

Legal Alignment: This is the final category of credible documentation. Do legal documents line up? According to the Federation of Independent Business Owners the top two threats to an owner's retirement from their business are 1) weak documentation and 2) owners' business plans misaligning with their personal estate documents.[61]

Misalignment is frequently the result of two separate advisors creating the plans without collaborative consultation or the failure to keep them simultaneously current. One example is when buy-sell agreements or stock certificate designations list how owner interests will be transferred while the owner's Last Will and Testament spells out a different designation or path. A second example can occur when the business owner's estate and business plan fail to align business ownership with the ownership of the real estate (the deed) upon which the business is located. Since the language on the deed trumps the language in a business agreement, a question of ownership will create red flags for valuation and future liabilities to a potential buyer or co-owner. It may also delay a close.

When you prepare your documentation, conduct a simple credibility test. Give it to a few trusted people who don't have a stake in the ownership transfer, such as your controller, CPA or legal advisors. The credibility issues may not be about veracity, but instead about clarity or ambiguity, missing data or even language. You believe you have skillfully connected the dots, but others may not see how this package gives a fair picture of your company. Probe their views, seek advice and then act on their recommendations.

Lacking credible performance, and legal documentation is like a road sign with flashing caution lights for you and prospective buyers. It flashes Road Hazard ahead! Now is the time to work closely with your legal, financial and tax advisors to ensure a complete and valid set of documents.

Bridge Actions: Assess your data and document availability and credibility.

1. Refine your data/document plan to identify what's in place or not and a timeline for getting everything gathered.

2. Assess the credibility of the numbers through a third party's validation, including compliance with GAAP guidelines.

3. Evaluate the currency and alignment of legal contracts, estate documents (wills, trusts) and corporate or partnership agreements.

4. Modify your administrative budget for the year; this task will create legal, accounting and other fees.

DEFINE SALES PROCESS AGREEMENTS

There are three main legal documents that protect you during the sales process: a Confidentiality or Non-disclosure Agreement, Letter of Intent and the Purchase/ Sales Agreement (contract of sale).

Confidentiality Agreement

A confidentiality agreement, which is signed by a prospective buyer, states that in examining your business they will not use the information they receive or uncover for any purpose other than making the decision to buy it. It defines at a minimum:

- The purpose for the non-disclosure, e.g., due diligence in the exploration of a purchase and the duration of the agreement
- What is considered confidential, e.g., information and material *shared or uncovered* that has or *could have* commercial value to the owner including proprietary processes a buyer may observe
- The limits of the non-disclosure, such as information that is in the public domain
- Who may access the information, such as the officers or advisors in the buyer's company
- Other boundaries, such as forbidding sharing that talks are even in progress

You, as well as a buyer, are obligated to assure confidentiality. For example, you must label shared documents as *Confidential* (electronically or in hard copy); state in your presentations that information shared is subject to the non-disclosure agreement; and direct what documents must be returned and when.

Letter of Intent

The letter of intent signifies the mutual interest that you and a prospective buyer have in completing a purchase transaction, through either shares in or the full acquisition of a business. It is *not a binding agreement*. It is an indication, however, of good faith and trust that you intend to come to agreement once the due diligence and negotiations are finished. It spells out:

- What is to be purchased or transferred, by whom to whom
- The proposed price and terms of the purchase and the conditions for the sale of the business
- The state whose laws govern the agreement
- The term of the agreement, i.e., when it expires
- Whether there are exclusive negotiation rights, such as a period when each side agrees to negotiate with no other parties

Purchase or Sales Agreement

This is the key document to finalize the purchase of the business. The U.S. Small Business Administration provides a checklist to be addressed in a small business sales agreement.[62] The sales agreement reflects the negotiated terms and conditions of the sale. It usually includes:

- The names of seller, buyer and business
- Assets to be included in the sale, such as business name, property, physical assets, contracts, I.P. and customer lists
- Purchase price and currency, e.g., stocks, cash, earnout
- Restraints, e.g., non-compete clauses
- The conditions and terms of the Agreement from Terms and Conditions Agreement

- Escrow requirements, representation and warranties of the seller and buyer
- Definition of how the business will be run prior to closing
- Contingencies, such as verification of financials, regulatory filings, financial terms and vehicles, security agreements and others
- Transition obligations, such as training, employment agreements and consolidations
- Fees, including brokers or M&A agent /banker's fees
- Date of closing

Closing Documents

There are a number of closing documents necessary for the close of the sale. These include, as appropriate:

Escrow Agreement:

This spells out the percentage of the purchase price held in reserve that will be paid to the seller after a specified period that protects the buyer from undisclosed liabilities or material changes, in the condition of assets.

Settlement or Closing Statement:

This can be as simple as a single page spreadsheet to a more complex several-page document listing the purchase price, the costs and price adjustments to be paid by and/or credited to the seller and buyer.

Security Agreements:

These are between a buyer and lender. They secure the debt against default and list the conditions of default.

Bill of Sale:

This is used more commonly in micro business and small business transfers, and, just like when selling your car, it confirms the transfer of title for your business with what terms.

Promissory Note:
This debt instrument is an alternative to a conventional bank loan. It is typically used where owner financing is involved, or no conventional financial institution can be used as a lender. It is the agreement between a lender and borrower, but unlike a simple IOU, it states not only the amount borrowed and when it is due, but also the steps required to pay back the debt and the consequences of default.

These agreements might make it feel like you must be guarded, distrustful and even adversarial in your sales transactions. Instead, these documents are like safety rails on your exit road. Even the most expert and cautious drivers need them when the tire blows on a steep mountain road. Your goal is to use them to keep on a road free of financial catastrophe at worst and from emotional wear and tear at a minimum.

REVIEW COMPANY LEGAL AGREEMENTS

There are legal entity documents you need to review with your advisors early in your exit planning. The agreements define your legal business entity structure, to whom you may sell and by what rules. They can be either helpful or obstructions if they are not attended to in the process of exit planning.

Legal Entity Documents

The best legal entity structure for your business was decided when you started your company. However, as you consider the transfer of ownership either to an internal or external buyer or through an IPO, the rules for partnerships versus LLC versus sole proprietorships or S/C corporations will demand different actions and pose different restraints. For example, your legal entity designation will affect who can be an eligible buyer and the tax consequences of the sale. The sooner these implications are understood in the timeline of exiting your business, the more freedom you have to modify the structure if needed.

My former company faced a significant challenge to a major growth opportunity due to its legal entity designation. We needed an Australia base with an Australian partner to work with three major new clients. This new partner would also round out the ownership team by buying a block of shares in the business. But, as an S Corp we could not sell an interest in our business to a foreign national. We had to convert to an LLC entity to realize the growth opportunity, increase the value of our business and meet my exit plan. With our lawyer and CPA, we were able to make the conversion well in advance of my exit and accelerate our growth and the value of the business.

Operating Agreements

Operating Agreements go by several names depending upon the legal entity. S Corporations have shareholder agreements; LLCs have operating agreements, and Partnerships have partnership agreements. These are not a purchase agreement between owners and buyers as in a real estate contract. Instead, these control the transfer of ownership interests when an owner leaves the business. This can be stipulated in a number of ways: a member's retirement, a disability, divorce, resignation or termination; an offer from someone to purchase an owner's interest in the company; a foreclosure of a debt secured by an owner's interests, including bankruptcy.

This agreement defines the answers to the following business questions:

- What events trigger a buyout? For example, is there a minimum tenure or a retirement age?
- Who may buy a departing owner's share in the business? What are the obligations of the remaining owners to purchase shares or allow the sale to a third party?
- What rights have shareholders, in the sale of an interest or the business, e.g., right of first refusal?
- What valuation will determine the value of the company and with what payment terms?

An LLC was experiencing conflict over the exit of a partner. As I listened to the turmoil, all parties kept referring to their operating agreement as if it was the Holy Grail for how to proceed. Each party recited the terms as if they were reading from different documents. When I asked how long it had been since they had reviewed or revised them, the answer was, "Not in the last 10 years." This length of time encompassed more than half the history of the company.

Review and update this agreement periodically with your advisors and well in advance of exiting your business so they reflect changes in your business, external realities and changes in the law. You also must update it to make sure multiple owners mutually understand it.

At the risk of sounding like a broken record, don't try to figure this out on your own. The penalty is high if you get it wrong.

In Conclusion

Gearing up for the sale simply means preparing yourself for and protecting yourself in the selling process. Selling your business is time consuming and a distraction to your usual routine and focus. It also requires diligence that your interests are protected legally. Don't skip this step and don't delay starting.

GEAR UP FOR THE SALE

Prepare to divert 30-60 percent of your time away from running your business to selling it. The time demanded accelerates, as you get closer to a sale.

Protect yourself during the sales process. Make sure the following are in place:
- Informational documents
- Sales process agreements
- Legal entity documents are current and executed

Your Data Bank substantiates your value, salability and your management transparency. Make sure it is complete, accurate, believable, accessible and internally consistent.

SCENIC OVERLOOK

GEARING UP TOOLS

This Scenic Overlook provides you with worksheets to begin to look at how ready you are to put up the For Sale sign from the standpoint of information and documentation. Your goal is to make sure the following are in place: Informational documents, Sales process agreements, and Legal entity documents.

You will also begin to define your Data Bank to substantiate your value and provide management transparency. You will assess to what degree your data and documents are complete, accurate, believable, and internally consistent.

I. PREPARE YOUR DOCUMENTATION

A. Create Your Story

Directions:

For each area below, build YOUR company story. What are the main points you want to make for each category. What evidence (data, compelling example or anecdote) will best support your points? You may want to use a separate page to write your answers for each of the six areas. For a larger list of factors refer to the Selling Memo in this chapter.

Consider using the same framework to sit in the shoes of a potential buyer and list what other areas they will request in their due diligence work. Don't omit this step for internal buyers. You want them to be fully informed about the current state of and forecast for the business they will lead.

Key Points	Evidence
Financial Strength	
Growth Potential	
Synergies	
People	
Brief History	
Selling Objectives	

B. Define Your Data Bank:

Directions:

1. Let this list be your starting point. Check which of these you need for representing your business to a buyer. Write in any others given your unique circumstances.

2. What are your priorities and the timeline for creating a data bank? Your list should cover the basic four major categories: financial, growth, legal and market/sales and others specific to your company.

• Historical earnings • Working capital and capital expenditure requirements • Budgets and cash flows • Revenue forecasts, • Accounts payable and receivable data • Payroll, with wage/salary costs • Historical and projected business trends • Strategy and vision • Competitive advantage data • _____ • _____	• Bench strength and resumes • Demographics and headcount breakdowns • Technology and intellectual property assets • Operating metrics, e.g., capacity utilization, sales per person, customer churn, product pipeline • Legal agreements, e.g., employment, purchase, sale or issuance of securities • _____ • _____	• Compliance certifications unique to the business such as EEOC, EPA, OSHA • Contingent liabilities, such as • Contracts and agreements, warranty guarantees and product liability, unfunded past service costs, e.g., retirement benefits • Real estate, leases and insurance, assets and liabilities • _____ • _____

C. Ensure Data and Document Credibility

Directions:

1. Enter your priorities from the previous list. Then rate how well it will meet the criteria listed to the right

1= high-risk area 3= could be stronger 5= passes clean audit test or 100 percent complete

Performance Data	Complete	Accurate	Believable
Financial Current and Historical			
• • •			
Growth Forecast			
• • •			
Market and Customer			
• • •			
Legal			
• • •			

Actions called for are...	The person responsible is...
1.	
2.	
3.	

D. Review Personal Financial Plans and Legal Documents

Directions:

1. Describe the state of the following set of plans and agreements.

2. List the issues that exist for these plans, e.g., date of last review; changes in ownership or health/marital status of owners or key talent; significant changes in economic conditions.

3. Define actions required.

Financial Review

Plans	Exists? (Y/N)	Currency Issues
a. Estate Plan		
b. Key person insurance		
c. Personal financial plan		
d. Personal and company tax strategy		
e. Plan to monetize business - pull equity or convert to cash		

Legal Agreements Review

Agreement	Exists? (Y/N)	Currency Issues (last reviewed?)
a. Shareholder or Operating Agreement or their equivalent		
b. Letter of Intent		
c. Confidentiality agreement		
d. Key talent retention agreements		

Action Plans: _____

_____

_____

THIRD AND FINAL LEG

LETTING GO WITH SERENITY

STEP 8 ~ LEAD YOUR WAY OUT

Nothing is secure but life, transition, and the energizing spirit.

Ralph Waldo Emerson

In working with companies large and small, private and public, I have been frustrated when I hear the following kinds of comments about an impending transfer of ownership:

"They said there would be no changes and then …"

"I haven't a clue what makes this place run and I'm supposed to become a partner?"

"My son never wanted to run the business, but he bought it for his wife to keep it in the family."

and finally,

"We were sold down the river."

Transferring ownership is typically a destabilizing event charged with emotion and ambiguity. It needs your leadership. In your final leg of the exit journey, *Letting Go with Serenity,* you examine transition leadership – YOURS. You'll be asking some hard questions of yourself, such as how effective am I at letting go? Letting go means you feel there are enough controls and plans in place that, upon your exit, your business will do just fine without you. How will you transfer the reins? And finally, what will goodbye look like?

This step, *Lead Your Way Out,* looks specifically at the human side of leaving and what it takes to lead your ownership transfer to a successful conclusion. *Leading* actually began in Step 1. You led when you defined your exit goals for yourself and your business. You led when you built a strong team of advisors and when you faced reality, identified obstacles to salability and then tuned-up the business.

The statistics on transfers are not encouraging. In family owned businesses, fewer than half make it to generation two and only about 12 percent make it to generation three.[63] While three out of four businesses consider succession a priority, fewer than 40 percent of those have implementation plans which, as you know, is a value driver and salability factor.[64] You, personally, are also experiencing a transition. Turning over power and ownership redefines your role in life. Step 8 reduces the chance you will be one of the many owners who regret selling their businesses because they did not consider the end game and how to manage it.

This step may feel like a route change from the technical work of valuation, legal agreements and salability. It is more like moving into an express lane that accelerates progress. This leg is fueled by your values and a bias for action. If you are like many mid and late-stage career business owners, you value inclusion, teamwork, innovative thinking and results. As you exit, you want to "do what's right" for your people, customers and suppliers. The challenge for you is not finding out what is right but choosing *how to lead well* given those values.

LEAD THE TRANSITIONS

What are we trying to accomplish when leading exit transitions?

- The first is communicating that the business is ready to be sold, and your people are capable of carrying on after you leave. The next three outcomes help accomplish the first.
- Your priorities and vision for the company and your exit are known and understood by your key stakeholders.
- There are clear expectations for accountability for accomplishing transition objectives.
- There is sustained commitment to your business and minimum anxiety about the future.

An important benefit of leading your transition well is that your buyer sees a company ready for an ownership change minus the traffic jams that many transfers experience. They see a transition being managed proactively with accountability, and people who are ready to carry on after your departure.

So what do change leaders do to achieve these outcomes? When I consulted with a Fortune 100 company cited as the "most change adaptable company" of the decade, I spent most of my time working with leaders on how to lead accelerated change. We built a framework to explain what successful change leaders do to achieve their desired outcomes. The framework translates easily to leading an Exit Strategy in a closely held private company.

Leaders of private businesses spend *time and attention* on their exit plan; they prioritize the work and make it *legitimate* through resource support, and they *engage* others to build ownership in the change. What does that look like?

Pay Personal Attention

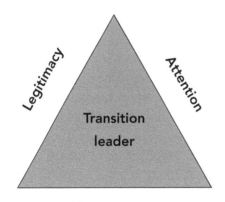

The average executive spends less than 12 minutes on a task before being interrupted or moving on, so that allocation of time is the signal for what is important. What leaders attend to is what gets done. Unfortunately, many spend time on what is urgent, not always what is important. Legend has it that David Kearns, former CEO of Xerox, was asked to total the time he spent on a Baldrige Award initiative he had committed to his Board to achieve. He was spending less than 10 percent of his month on it. He was advised to stop the initiative unless he could more than double the allocation. He did. They won.

If you believe your exit strategy and tune-up plans are important and will improve the likelihood of a profitable exit and a sustainable company, then you must be seen with your hands on the wheel, not holding a stopwatch on others. You work your exit plan and keep it on the agenda quarter to quarter. You allocate and protect time on your calendar for exit work versus *fitting it in* when there is slack on the calendar. In the previous step, you were advised to adjust your calendar to provide time for the selling tasks. In this step, you consider what adjustments are needed for transition tasks such as improvement projects, succession or customer and revenue retention.

Legitimize and Provide Resources

People know what is important by what resources you allocate to projects or functions, (your time as well as budget dollars.) One way to legitimize the work required in your exit strategy is to make sure it is based on your reality check and linked to operating objectives such as growth, productivity and control. When you put some of your best people on key transition tasks such as improving financial reporting systems or defining retention strategies for key customers and employees, you make those tasks legitimate. When you stay the course and monitor progress on exit tasks – as you would for other important business projects – you make this work real.

Engage Others in the Transition

By identifying ways to engage your people in driving continuity plans involving, for example, key customers, key process improvements or on merger integration teams, you transfer the reins and widen responsibility for making a stronger company. It's true; those who build things feel ownership for their continuation. Finally, when your people feel engaged and see colleagues involved, they have a greater feeling of control. This minimizes anxiety and productivity-drift during exit transitions, improves retention of key talent and minimizes customer anxiety and churn.

UNDERSTAND BOTH POWER AND ASSET TRANSFERS

An effective continuity plan addresses two kinds of transfers: *assets* or wealth and *power.*

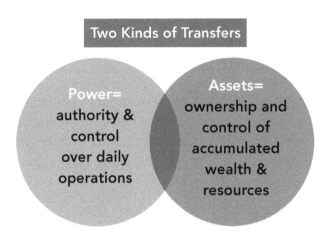

The transfer of *assets* means moving the wealth that has been accrued or concentrated in the business to designated partners, heirs, employees or external buyers.

The transfer of *power* means transitioning control over the business' daily operation to those capable and ready to exercise it whether they are internal or external people, buyers or not.

It is important to recognize that these two types of transfers are separate but equal in importance. They may also be independent of each other; in other words, the wealth of the company may be transferred to an entity different from those who assume the day-to-day power of leading the business. This is most obvious in sales to private equity firms or an acquiring company.

It is an important distinction also in family-owned businesses where the second generation may exercise increasing control (leadership power) long before a complete transfer of assets occurs. Differentiating the type of transfer will allow you to create a distinct bridge plan for each case.

The following sections describe the typical "potholes" that can make for a rough ride in transferring assets and power. Each section describes the pothole, then the bridging actions or plans that help you avoid a rough road.

PLAN YOUR ASSET TRANSFERS AND AVOID THEIR POTHOLES

There are three big *potholes* that can cause a rough ride in transferring assets. If you see or anticipate them, you must develop a bridge plan over or around them. The first two are poor seller due diligence and weak preparation of managers/family. The third, lack of succession planning, is not a pothole but a sink hole! It impacts asset and power transfers and is discussed in detail in Plan for Power Transfers section, and in Appendix C.

Pothole 1: *Inadequate* Seller *Due Diligence*

Only 16 percent of all letters of intent are eventually consummated in a company sale, and in the majority of cases, the issue is the quality of the buyer and poor seller due diligence.[65] Despite the time spent on it, it is often poorly done because the checklist is incomplete and dominated by buyer requirements. The seller spends an enormous amount of time preparing responses to a buyer's needs regarding the financials, bench strength, product and revenue pipelines, and metrics on market share, customer bases, and the list goes on.

However, there is also a *seller* due diligence checklist on potential buyers. The due diligence unique to the seller involves a) qualifying the financial strength of a buyer to close the deal, b) learning the buyer's goals, reputation for pre- and post-close behavior and c) evaluating the buyer's operating philosophy and company culture for compatibility.

Financial Strength: You need to know, for example, the financial strength and solvency of the buyer) including where the buyer is getting the investment capital and under what terms; if there is a history of warrants and heavy conditions in previous purchase agreements and their track record in closing a deal, e.g., on time and without last minute surprises. A mining company was selling an asset and, at the closing, the buyer arrived with insufficient funds expecting the owner to grant a hardship discount. The seller later discovered this was a well-practiced act.

Goals and Reputation: Here you want to know the buyer's objectives, e.g., strategic integration or growth/ROI). Is this a fit with your growth strategy, customers and people? Whether a prospective buyer is an individual, a competitor or a larger company, be sure to understand their strategy and philosophy. For example, is this a vertical integration for them? Are they buying customers? Are they buying the talent, technology or I.P. and don't plan to keep the whole package? Do they want to add capabilities, products or markets that they don't have? Knowing their strategy will determine the degree to which you can negotiate agreements that support the continuity of your suppliers, customers and talent. Which of their goals will allow you to leave with serenity and a legacy of sustainability for your people and your customers?

What is the buyer's reputation for pre- and post-close behavior? Do they live up to verbal agreements in the final terms and conditions? Do they follow through on transition plan agreements such as talent retention or supplier relationships?

Operating Philosophy and Culture Fit: Operating philosophy consists of those strong convictions we have, such as what motivates people, what is good management and what drives value and customer loyalty. Explore these beliefs because they drive behaviors. Probe a buyer, for example, on their short fuses or greatest current challenge. Their answers usually illustrate their values.

When I asked a former owner of a successful retail cancer care product business how the sale of her company went, she replied, "Great, except I sold it to the wrong buyer." She regretted that she had not looked into the buyer's management and customer practices in more detail versus relying on the buyer's story. Within one year of the sale, the new buyer had replaced the entire experienced staff with retail hourly workers. The heart of the business, it's reputation for knowledgeable, personalized customer care, evaporated.

If a private equity firm is your likely buyer/investor, then knowing their operational philosophy and how they plan to involve you (or not) with company operations will help you create a workable post-purchase transition plan.

With internal ownership transfers and family succession, the questions are similar but often phrased differently. What is the leadership style of the successor? What are they known for, e.g., customers first? Growth, above all else? Lifestyle and status? Teamwork? Are they perceived as "just like the boss" (i.e., you) or "couldn't be more different?" What are the implications for leading the transition? Past performance and behavior in leaders is a predictor of future behavior, unlike stock picks.

Stay in touch with your intuition, that feeling that something isn't quite right even if you can't name it. In one company's sale, the buyer CEO repeatedly failed to attend face-to-face meetings with the seller despite agreeing to be there each time. The seller called the deal off sensing there was an integrity issue. Was it a subjective evaluation? Absolutely. Did the seller regret the decision? No.

Culture conflicts, in addition to being the number one cause of failed mergers and acquisitions, are often at the heart of what is called *post-merger slump,* a period of 12 months on average, where productivity takes a dive along with morale. If you have an earn-out or installment package as part of the deal, this productivity loss effects your payout. Knowing the culture fit and developing a transition plan that considers culture can mitigate or shorten the slump, improve your legacy and preserve your financial goals.

Getting the right price is a key goal in your sale. So is your serenity in knowing you have done your best to leave your people, your customers and your business in good hands.

Bridge Actions:
1. Bridging the gap in seller due diligence involves defining a protocol in advance of putting up the for-sale sign. Define the information and data you require of the potential buyer. Research the financial viability of a buyer. Identify how you will be represented in acquiring the information you need, such as a broker or an outside advisor.

2. Use multiple approaches (triangulate the data) including person-to-person interactions so you have a chance for a gut check and don't only rely on reports from a buyer.

3. For internal transfers, conduct a 360° review of key successors to identify philosophy, leadership style, strengths and any warning signs.

Pothole 2: Weak Preparation of Managers or Family for the Change
It's critical that you prepare your managers or family owners for the sale of your company; but isn't that obvious? In fact, in acquisitions and mergers that failed to meet their objectives, almost 90 percent of managers reported being uninformed of the impending acquisition or plans for the post-close period.[66]

Conventional wisdom states that you don't discuss the sale until you have a signed deal. In fact, poor communication with employees has a greater detrimental effect on deal success than poor communication to shareholders, suppliers or customers. When you make communications a priority during an ownership transition, you are more likely to be successful than the average company in a merger or acquisition.[67] I have seen three approaches to communicating with and preparing managers for a sale.

Say Nothing: The advice of many brokers reinforces the belief that we should say nothing prior to having a letter of intent. Then we can make an announcement to top management eliciting codes of silence. The fear is that disclosure fuels speculation, turnover and disruption of work. However, it is also true that when there is inadequate information but a robust rumor mill, people feel anxious, worry about job security, feel a loss of control and even abandonment – something akin to being *sold down the river*. People look for ways to regain control as with getting their resume up-to-date and activating their professional network. In fact, appropriate information *decreases* feelings of vulnerability and increases a sense of control. Below is one example of this approach and its consequences.

> A small business owner sold his business of 25+ years and informed his small family of staff when the deal was about to be signed. He had feared they might leave if he told them earlier. (One stipulation of the sales contract was that the two lead sales staff must remain in place with two-year non-compete agreements). When the two sales leads got the news their response was predictable: anger from being left in the dark and then asking, "So what's in it for me?" to be part of this. To ensure the close, the owner negotiated a hefty "stay bonus" from his proceeds of the sale. In the year following the close, sales fell 25 percent. Maybe this was due to the economy or to the leadership style of the new owner, or perhaps it was from the scar tissue that had formed on those key employees.

A second fear is that if employees learn you are selling the company, the information will leak out to customers and competitors who will undermine the value of the business. Some advisors suggest using a cover story to tell employees for when strange people are seen in plants and offices. The cover story goes like this:

"We are looking for new financing for strategic growth opportunities and holding discussions with various…blah blah…" However, once the full story is learned (and it will be), the damage is done to management trust and credibility and your legacy takes a hit.

Tell All: The total opposite approach is *Tell Everyone Everything*. The advantage is it shortcuts the rumor mill when everyone hears the same message, especially if there is a Q&A period. However, there are downsides with this option:

- You lose control over information dissemination beyond those in the room;
- You can set up unrealistic expectations about what will be communicated to whom and how frequently;
- Everyone cannot digest everything, nor is it recalled accurately;
- You can never tell everything because some things must remain confidential, and you don't know the answers to everything that everyone will have questions about!

Tell All and Say Nothing strategies have more potential for downside effects than upside.

Thoughtful Transparency: The third option is called Thoughtful Transparency. Here you disclose your intention to sell, your timeframe and something of the rationale and fit with the company strategy. Perhaps key leaders receive a more complete briefing including a profile of the desired buyer: what the process will entail and how they may be involved. This group will want interaction with you and guidance about cascading information (what and to whom and when) and how to protect the sales process.

For example, the CEO of a 50-person financial software tools company held key management and all-staff meetings to share his plan to sell the business, how it fit the vision and strategy of the company and the preferred buyer profile. He called it a "controlled conversation." People learned what kind of information they could expect, and what would not be shared and why. Those closest to customers knew how to deliver consistent messages about the strategy and philosophy of the sale. The transparency of the process was congruent with their belief that if you "treat people like responsible adults, they will act like responsible adults." During the year-long process, no customers were lost; not a single staff member left nor did productivity decline.

I also spoke to a company owner who in a period of twelve years bought over 40 companies that he merged into one. He talked about preparing managers for the acquisition transitions and the power of transparency and involvement.

In one acquisition, he found that the top sales managers all planned to leave shortly after the sale. He had his own executive team but did not want to lose these sales leaders. So, *before* the close, these managers were given information about the long-term strategy and business model of the combined business. They were given the opportunity to invest modestly in the business (with a compensation plan that funded the buy-in). The transparency about the future, their role and importance in it and the payoff to them, resulted in all buying into the vision and ownership.

The key communication principles for you are 1) be clear about your philosophy and your goals based on your situation and 2) develop a communications plan for your each of your constituencies. A planning template is in Step 6 Scenic Overlook.

Bridge Actions:
1. Plan your communications strategy. If your goals are to prepare your people, provide a sense of control, and instill respect for you as an owner, then arrange for sufficient transparency about the process and be open to their questions and concerns.

2. Find a buyer with a compatible communication philosophy; they need to be on the same page about preparing your leaders.

MASTER THE UNIQUE CHALLENGES OF FAMILY ASSET TRANSFERS

Imagine you are some years younger and driving down the road with your parents in a truly classic car that has been in the family for decades. Mom tells you that they have decided to cash in on the value of the car. Your reaction might be:

- Support for the idea because you have never been a car aficionado
- One of concern that this valuable asset will leave the family estate
- Surprise and anger that they seem to have made this decision without consulting you—even though you have personally helped preserve and maintain the car for years.

If this tale sounds irrelevant to selling a business consider this: a survey of Canadian and U.S. family-owned businesses found that 73 percent of business owners stated they had not discussed the transfer of ownership of their business with the next generation.

Ownership Succession Planning

Families are complicated. The psychological dimensions of families and their companies make transition planning and ownership transfer complex and challenging. As Robin Klemm of Oregon State University stated, "Family businesses are as agile within a generation as they are fragile across generations."[69]

Conflicts between first and second-generation family members or among siblings are among the most difficult and important factors preventing intra-family transfer of ownership or causing an unplanned sale to an outside buyer. The fictionalized TV family businesses cannot compare to the true-life wars of the founding Mondavi brothers or the 68-years feud of second generation siblings that led to splitting their grandfather's and father's business in two—Adidas and Puma. Fortunately, there are examples of fourth-generation businesses successfully carrying on profitably as with Rain Bird Irrigation.

There was a time when families might have said, "*it goes without saying* that our son (or sometimes daughter) will take over the business when we retire." It was the default option. This is not as true today. Only 53 percent of business owners expect their company to remain in the family. [70]

Perhaps the hardest task in family asset transfers are those hard discussions that include emotional subjects like grandpa's eventual passing, or who is best suited take the reins or ownership dispersion and capital distributions.

There are four topics to address and reach closure on in family ownership transfers. Each of the four topics has a set of questions to be answered. These are touched on briefly here because it is a subject extensively written about elsewhere by specialists in family enterprise management. If your family business is complicated, consider adding a family enterprise specialist to your advisory team.

Strategy, vision and values: What legacy values and operating principles are at the core of your company and who best personifies them? What is your vision for the future and does he/she believe in it and aspire to it?

Passages and their timing: One of the toughest conversations for intergenerational ownership is the discussion about death and retirement. Are there contingency plans in place (not to mention key man insurance and estate documents) for the sudden passing of an owner? Are there criteria for retirement and descriptions of post transfer roles? Is death the milestone for ownership transfer?

Roles and boundaries: What are the key roles for operating, governing and participating in this business? How are these tied to asset holdings? What are the boundaries (rights and obligations) of these roles? What are the capabilities of those who would fill them? As the family grows with each generation, what are the decision rules and mechanisms to follow? What skills will this require of those in governance roles? Who has them now?

Ownership dispersion and capital distribution options: How will ownership shares be distributed from generation to generation both in quantity and timing? Will distribution be a result of certain milestones in the company or personal to the beneficiary, e.g., at a certain age?

This list of questions shape the agenda for a series of advisor and family meetings. You must prepare for these by getting clear on what decisions are yours, which involve others (and who), what information will make for good decision-making, and your tolerance for and skill in dealing with debate and possible conflict.

Ownership Roles and Relationships

The ownership roles in family succession planning vary. Examples include a family member in a completely passive role (a shareholder with no governance or employee status); a shareholder and employee; a shareholder in a governance role but not an employee (perhaps a first generation owner who is Board Chair but no long CEO); an employee but not a shareholder (as with a non-family member in a management role). Defining these roles as the dispersion of ownership grows, e.g., to the cousin generation, makes asset transfers in succession planning more difficult than in non-family-owned businesses.

There are many ways to look at this transition ranging from the simple family tree to a narrative story to a succession map. Your goal is to clarify your thinking about asset transfer and the roles of heirs in your business. What is clear to you and what are your nagging questions? Meet with your financial and estate planners to help clarify your thinking and know your options.

Bridge Actions:

1. As the head of your family business, you must be clear about what is non-negotiable and what is open to input or joint decision-making in advance of announcing your retirement or a change of command. In other words, make the *rules of engagement* clear on such central asset and power transfer subjects as external sale of assets versus internal succession transfer, timing and transition events/milestones and criteria for succession.

2. Touch Time: The most important bridgework you do as a leader is to have the conversation with your family and potential successors about the future of the business, career interests and the profile of higher leadership positions. These are discussions visited periodically versus three months before you decide to leave/retire.

3. Establish a Succession Development **process** for internal managers or family owners. This is discussed in more detail as we delve into continuity planning for successors later in this chapter.

PLAN YOUR <u>POWER</u> TRANSITIONS AND AVOID THEIR POTHOLES

Let's move from the transfer of business *assets* and ownership to the challenges and best practices of transferring *power,* turning over the reign and the reins.

Why differentiate power transfer from asset transfer? This is done because one does not necessarily follow the other. The power to execute the day-to-day business may remain with company management after it is sold even though they have no share of ownership. Likewise, the transfer of assets to several siblings in a family business may not include appointing them to management or governance of the business. Making power transfer explicit is the subject of this transition and set of bridge plans.

There are two important potholes on the road to your transfer of power. The first is understanding the power of the leadership culture to influence the sustainability of your business. The second is the process by which we identify and develop successors to take on power whether they will be owners or not.

Pothole 1: Underestimating the Power of the Leadership Culture

As discussed in Step 3, culture plays a key role in the perceived *salability* of your company as well as its *sustainability.* Studies have shown that leadership culture affects productivity, sales and market responsiveness.[71] Here is one example of its bearing on sustainability post-close.

I was asked to do a *postmortem* assessment of an acquired scientific and engineering firm. The acquired company (100 percent owned by its CEO with about 90 employees) had lost almost 70 percent of its top key talent in the first year after the sale. And, every few months, there would be a crisis requiring parent company intervention. The parent company had believed the acquired company's founder would play an advisory role for one year. They assumed that talented technical people would be the day-to-day leaders. Instead, the talented technical people were leaving.

What we discovered was a leadership philosophy that rewarded fire fighting over prevention. It was a culture that promoted arsonists! This allowed the founder to maintain control and continue his reign. The founder did not see himself as the advisor but rather as the decider. His technical leaders believed the leadership style would change with the acquisition. The frustration of these leaders led to a mass exodus in the first year. The parent company's original hands off transition plan switched to letting the former CEO go and inserting a new COO to oversee programs, rebuild the talent pool, and lead a culture change.

Bridge Actions:

Take a step back to evaluate and understand the existing leadership style in your company and its power over how things work and how it will sustain the health of the company after you leave. Doing this evaluation will allow you to define:

1. The actual leadership culture and assess its influence on company performance. There are several excellent online assessments that characterize and assess corporate cultures.

2. The desired profile of the next generation of leader and who currently fits that profile.

The purpose of an assessment is to identify how current leadership practices influence company value and the effective transfer of power. Your goal is to have a prospective buyer see your leadership culture as a valued asset, not a risk to sustainability.

Pothole 2 Weak Succession Planning

Peter Drucker said, "There is no success without a successor." No matter what list of exit strategy essentials you examine, succession planning is on it. This is also true for any book or blog on leadership focused on how to assess and develop leaders for the future. This wealth of information creates its own challenge. There is so much written and so many perspectives that it can feel daunting. Succession planning does not have to be daunting. But not tackling it has daunting consequences. Here are two examples.

During an interview with the identified successors in an engineering firm, I asked what it took to become a partner. Not one could name the criteria or the process, and none had a development plan to assume this role. When this fundamental information is lacking, there exists a sense of powerlessness over one's career, as in

"I guess it's out of my hands;" heightened risk aversion and decreased innovation, that sounds like, "I better not rock the boat;" and frustration and potential for loss of key talent as people believe, "I can do more elsewhere."

In another company, an MBA engineer hired for the explicit purpose of replacing a partner over a two-year period gave his notice. He cited two main reasons for his decision: the lack of a plan to transition responsibilities and authority from the exiting partner and failure to have a mentor to help him with his transition. The possible loss of this high-potential leader sounded the alarm that the partners' inattention to succession was threatening their exit strategy.

What makes this inattention typical? First, developing leaders is a long-range effort on a soft subject. The best development process begins years ahead of an exit when it doesn't feel as urgent as daily concerns, such as cost over-runs. The urgent almost always trumps the strategic. Second, good development is tied to strategy. When strategy is undeveloped, it is difficult to define the profile of the leader of the future. Third, leadership development requires conversations with key talent to understand their aspirations and career goals and how they fit the company's plans. These conversations are often avoided because they raise fears of making promises that might be difficult to keep.

What's the pay-off? At its best, succession development produces alignment. The son of a business owner disclosed that he always knew he wanted to lead his dad's company, and they had often spoken about the path forward. When the time was right, the transition was clear. On the other hand, the following is not unusual. A senior manager who had been identified as a partner successor confessed that he loved his company and his work. Then he added, "I am not sure I want to run it though." His boss, a partner, was in the dark about this view.

At its simplest, it has three phases: identification, grooming and appointment. Appendix C offers additional details on each phase with application tools and a worksheet. Here are four simple questions to begin your planning on the transfer of the reins.

Bridge Actions:

1. Do you know who your likely successors are?

2. Are they interested in this role?

3. Do they have development plans aligned with their goals and your needs?

4. What is their financial ability to become owners? What will enable this?

5. What would you be willing to hold back from being paid if the leadership you had in place left or failed soon after the close? In other words, would you bet a part of your payout on them given the current succession process you have in place?

In Conclusion

The most powerful element in a successful transfer of ownership is your leadership of the transitions involved. Your attention, support and engagement of others is key to your effectiveness. To successfully let go of control and the reins, you must lead the exit process around the predictable potholes.

The major outcomes of leading your exit transition well are that your business is ready to be sold, and people can carry on after you leave knowing the vision and strategy and their roles. People and customer anxiety is minimized, and they remain committed to your business.

LEAD YOUR WAY OUT

Great transition leaders do three things: Pay attention, legitimize projects and engage people in driving improvement.

Be alert for four Transfer Potholes: inadequate due diligence on your prospective buyer; weak preparation of your managers or family; underestimating the power of the leadership culture; and weak succession planning and development.

Family businesses have two difficult challenges: multi-generation succession planning and defining ownership roles.

SCENIC OVERLOOK

LEADING WELL EXERCISES

This Overlook presents tools for examining your transition leadership involved in asset and power transfers:

1. Leading transitions via a personal assessment and a calendar test

2. Letting go of the reins and old habits

Your goal is to gain a deeper understanding of how you want to lead this important phase in the life of your company. Knowing what habits might help you and hinder you, will let you more consciously lead. Knowing how you currently spend your time and how that picture might need to change during this transition period will let you pro-actively manage demands on your time. And finally, knowing how you can effectively transfer the reins of your business in advance of a new owner's arrival eases the transition for your people.

I. LEADING WELL

A. Transition Leadership Assessment

For each of the items in the three categories, consider your typical leadership behavior and how it will play out in leading and exit transition.

How Well Do You?	5= very well
A. Define reality, i.e., know what the state of the business is and its preparedness for sale? ____	3 =adequately
	1 =poorly
B. Pay attention to the exit strategy and plan? Seek and support transition tasks versus it's business as usual? ____	*Top area to*
C. Assign and clarify roles and responsibilities for key change or improvement initiatives? ____	*attend to:*
D. Demonstrate commitment – make the tough decisions to stay the course? Set a personal example for what is important? ____	
What Actions Will Likely be Taken?	5= very likely
E. Conduct a brutally honest readiness assessment. ____	3=maybe
F. Sponsor key exit transition tasks. ____	1=very unlikely
G. Manage personal time, energy and focus to be congruent with goals. ____	*Top area to*
	attend to:
H. Manage accountability and monitor the metrics; – i.e., stay the course. ____	
Where Might You Trip?	5= very likely
I. Don't match my exhortations and intentions with personal actions and rewards for early adopters. ____	3=maybe
J. Shift priorities or deplete resources from key exit tasks creating confusion. ____	1=very unlikely
	Top area to
K. Fail to integrate or link the exit strategy and continuity plans with the business operating plans. ____	*attend to:*
L. Inadequately engage my stakeholders' to promote capability and acceptance. ____	

So What? Now What?

- What are your personal potholes?

- Where will you get the biggest payoff if you make a change in your leadership practices?

- What and where can you start now?

B. Leadership Calendar Test

For the next two weeks, you are going to pay attention to where you are spending your time. This isn't a time to make excuses; in fact, it's the perfect time to analyze your time commitments and how you prioritize your activities.

Use the following chart as an example. (Make one and put it on your smart phone or other device.) Be faithful to your record keeping as each day passes. It's much easier to account for time as it's happening than having to account for it after-the-fact.

Activity	Mon	Tues	Wed	Thurs	Fri	Wkend	Total
Operations and Supply Chain Continuous Improvement Firefighting							
Customer Building relationships Firefighting							
Finance Receivables, Budgets, Project Reviews							
Strategy Product or Growth Plans et al Exit Plan							
People Development Problem solving							
Business Development – Marketing							
Product – Technology Development							
Other (specify)							
Total Hours per week							

So What? Now What? *When the two weeks are over, tally your time and ask yourself:*

- Does my time allocation match what I believe/say is important?

- If I continue spending my time in this way, what are the consequences to my exit strategy?

- What adjustments should I make? What can I start right away?

II. LETTING GO: ARE YOU REVVING THE ENGINE IN NEUTRAL?

One transition to manage is your role as a leader. The following questions focus on how you are promoting (or not) the development of others as leaders and decision-makers. A behavior trap is identified on the left with a corresponding behavior on the right. The goal of this exercise is to understand where you stand, so it's helpful to take it by yourself and also ask others whom you trust to answer the questions about you.

A. Tight Reins: Behavior Traps

The goal is to uncover the ways you can more effectively promote independent decision-making by what YOU do on a daily basis.

Leadership Trap	Ask Yourself to What Degree....
Micro-Managing	Am I bringing my people into the decision-making process appropriate to the situation and their career goals?
No Mistakes Risk Aversion	Am I willing to risk sharing the decision process enough for people to observe, participate and learn?
Crisis Management	To what extent do I respond late to issues thus creating an urgency or crisis that leads to directive decision-making? (i.e., "I have to decide.")
Looking for a Target	Do I focus more on targeting the blame than on understanding root causes or supporting problem-solving and learning?
Need to Know Information Flow	Am I willing to share information that will expand understanding of the business and confidence in independent decision-making?
Approachability	Do I invite and engage in informal communication with my people in order to build a sense of trust and collaboration?
Camouflage Decision Power	Do I work the decision with people until I get the answer I want?
Discouraging Dissent	How do I react when others disagree or challenge me? What percent of the time am I in a listening mode versus a telling/judging mode?

So What? Now What?

- Where are you strong in promoting independence and confident in others?

- Where could you be stronger?

- What could you stop doing or start doing that would change your effectiveness in growing people?

B. Tight Reins: Activity Traps

One of the most difficult behaviors for owners of closely held or family businesses is letting go of power – giving the steering wheel over to the next generation. The tool below helps you identify controlling habits and where opportunities for letting go exist.

- PART ONE: In each of the four **A** quadrants below, list three decisions, meetings, tasks or activities that you feel are yours. Those are areas that have been, and feel as though they need to be, yours. They often define your current daily pace and role.
- PART TWO: The **B** set of four-quadrants asks you why this is the way it *is/has always been* and to list what you could <u>let go</u> of in order to develop your potential successors.

Now here's the hard truth:

If you can't find ways to effectively let go, you cannot easily sell your business.

3 Approvals

3 key subjects on which you need to give your approval to people who work directly with/for you or to other key talent

1.
2.
3.

3 Meetings

3 important meetings that you must attend that only you can participate in

1.
2.
3.

I Hold On To

3 Critical Tasks

3 tasks only you can do, because of your technical proficiency, knowledge of the subject or tradition

1.
2.
3.

3 Activities

3 activities you would like to engage in today to energize yourself, yet for which you feel you have no time

1.
2.
3.

3 Approvals

Why must you approve it – their lack of knowledge?, skill?, time?, perceived risk? other?

_____

_____

_____

3 Meetings

Why can't they attend? Lack of knowledge or information?, lack of skill?, lack of time?, other? "Let Go" strategy/actions

_____

_____

_____

I Let Go

3 Tasks

Why don't they have the expertise? Where can they get it? "Let Go" strategy/actions

_____

_____

_____

3 Activities

Why can't you find the time? lack of discipline, fear of letting go, others' expectations/view of your role? other? "Let Go" strategy/actions

_____

_____

_____

After you have filled in the quadrants, ask yourself:

Easy to Change: Do it now.

1. _____

2. _____

3. _____

Develop a plan: Ease out of these activities.

1. _____

2. _____

3. _____

III. POWER POTHOLE FILLERS

A. Leadership Culture:

How confident are you that you know your company's leadership culture and how it affects your business performance, e.g., quality, growth, customer experience and operating efficiencies? How can you verify your perspectives?

- Our leaders impact our company performance because they consistently (describe actions or practices both plus and minus):

- What will a new owner most appreciate about our leadership culture? What might concern them?

- The aspects of leadership culture that must be in our company story are:

- One action I should consider reinforcing or strengthening in our leadership culture is:

B. Bench Strength & Succession:

To what degree is each of the following statements true?

1= not true at all ← —————————————→ 5= very true	Rating
We have defined the profile of the next generation of leaders for our company	____
We know who the high potential successors are for key leadership spots	____
Our people know what it takes to become a key leader in our company	____
We have plans in place to develop our successors, and they are monitored	____
The implications of these ratings for a successful power transfer are: Doing well, keep doing: Start doing or do more:	

IV. ASSET POTHOLE FILLERS

A. Manager Preparation

What will best prepare your key people for the sale of your company? Write down how you think and what you know about the following areas. How do they shape your philosophy on communication and involvement?

- What I am known for as a leader, my values, are

- To be congruent with my values when I communicate I should

- I have these assumptions and beliefs about my managers and people, e.g., loyalty, tolerance for ambiguity, integrity (as in they do what they say they will do).

- My concerns or beliefs about sharing information are

- The legal requirements I must follow, if any, are

- How effective and powerful is our rumor mill? What influence is it likely to have on my messages?

Overall, my communication *philosophy* is:

My engagement strategy might be:

- my target group is

- the best way to engage them is

- my timing and focus

B. Seller Due Diligence

What do you know and what does your intuition say about a prospective buyer in each of the following areas?

	Knowledge/Facts	Intuition Says
Financial Strength		
Buyer Goals		
Reputation		
Operating Philosophy & Culture		

What needs to happen to assure your comfort level with this buyer or move to another option?

STEP 9 ~ ANTICIPATE LIFE POST-DEPARTURE

I don't want to achieve immortality through my work ...
I want to achieve immortality through not dying.

Woody Allen

WHO ARE YOU IF NOT YOUR COMPANY?

I have an elderly mother who recently had to stop driving and sell her car. She learned to drive when she was over 30. Driving her first car was a moment that shaped her identity as an independent, modern woman able to navigate her world. Now that symbol was being stripped away. While there were alternate transportation options for getting around town, she couldn't see or accept them. Alternatives could not overcome her belief that she was no longer in control of life nor productive.

Your business, like Mom's car, can define your identity. It gives you meaningful goals and the satisfaction of seeing their accomplishment. It can give you a feeling of being needed for ideas and input, for leadership and decisions and for recognition. It gives you power and social standing. It can also give you a sense of control that your time – a day, a quarter, a year, – has a purpose, a schedule and a rhythm.

It is not surprising to learn that 75 percent of business owners regret selling their businesses after only one-year post-sale.[72] Some owners felt they sold too early and left money on the table. For others, seeing what had changed in their business after their departure or missing their colleagues was painful. Too many felt lost in the transition from a past that provided a clear sense of identity to an undefined future. There is not a small business owner I know who has not struggled with the question of post-exit identity at some time. The truth is, leaving your business no longer allows for that blurry distinction between you and your company.

After leaving a business there is a shift that changes the map of daily life: from your *business* providing the structure, purpose, challenge and rewards of daily life to the *choices you make* providing those things. This raises uncomfortable questions. Some questions are practical. How will I fill my day if I'm not at the office? Others questions are existential. Who am I, and what will give me meaning once I am no longer in this role and this business?

You give your business this power to define you and your time; most of us do. Just as a parent who can no longer drive must redefine how to have control over their mobility, your challenge is to take back the power over what it looks like to be meaningfully engaged.

Facing the question, "Who am I if not my company?" is an act of courage. You reflect, question and digest your life for the insights about what drives you: achievement, being needed or liked, power and control, recognition, compassion for others. This knowledge provides a tether that connects the power of the past, what satisfied and motivated you, to the power of the future, what characterizes your next endeavors. Without such insights, you will likely avoid exit planning, or just as serious, you will exit off the high-speed autobahn of being a *business owner* to a meandering back road lacking interest, direction or meaning.

The work you do in this step helps you understand your emotional response to endings, how to honor the past, and reach closure.

Endings are Emotional

Company leaders usually have three mindsets about selling and leaving their companies. Which of these resonates with you? A clue will be in your gut reaction to one or more of these mindsets.

You may see leaving as the equivalent of facing your *mortality*. The nightmare sounds like, "I went from being in 'Who's Who' to being 'Who?'" It's not surprising that to avoid confronting The End, chief executives do less end-of-career planning than non-executives.

You may have a sense of *completion*. You've accomplished your life's mission and are leaving a legacy, whether it's leaving a strong company to the next generation or providing financial security to your family. Your immortality is defined by what continues after your departure. It's one of the goals of owners who use Exit Signs as a roadmap for the exit planning.

You may see post-departure as a time of *rebirth* or an *encore*—an opportunity to connect with a new or unfulfilled higher purpose giving you a renewed sense of meaning. A recent survey showed how many people are considering a renewal or encore phase in retirement. Nine million of the estimated 100 million 45- to 70-year-olds are currently in encore careers; 31 million are interested in this career shift; and 27 percent desire to make the shift in the next five years.[74] If this is you, you're in a growing group.

Late career business owners who I interviewed all struggled with the question of "what comes after?" They did not have it all figured out in advance but were dealing with the ambiguity. They did not let their anxieties about the unknown paralyze them. Perhaps, as a result, they avoided Mark Twain's observation when he said, "I am an old man, and I have known a great many troubles, but most of them have never happened." These owners seemed to fall into three emotional states:

a. **Anticipation** This is the "I can't wait" group. These owners see a yet-undefined next adventure with no fully formed vision, but a belief that discovering it would, in itself, be part of the rewards of the next chapter. They exit the highway confident they will find an interesting road sign inviting them to explore new territory.

b. **Anxiety** is the second emotional state. It stems from having so many hopes about post-departure life but a lack of clarity about priorities, resources and how to meeting the diverse interests of family and friends This is the "how will

I decide?" group. They exit their career highway at a major juncture with signs pointing in many directions, all compelling and a bit confusing. They have to sort through their many choices.

c. **OMDB, aka Over My Dead Body** is the group who believes that to exit means driving to the junkyard or the old folks' home, and they aren't going there! They haven't chosen to let anticipation or anxiety fuel forward motion but choose instead to slam on the brakes or shove the car in reverse. This choice, however, increases the likelihood that they will find themselves stalled in a parking lot waiting for someone to *take them somewhere and* feeling they've lost control.

Mindset fuels behavior and energy as demonstrated below.

When a good friend exited his business in a liquidation event, he was not prepared. For a while, he tried to re-engage in his field as a specialist/consultant. He experienced a growing depression. Then, his daughter announced she was expecting his first grandchild. His initial reaction was not joy. It was a deeper depression over the idea of being *old*. He recalled his grandfather as old and in a nursing home. But when he held his grandson for the first time, he made a mental shift. He moved from his job defining his importance to defining his own meaning and importance. He decided his new role was to mentor and make a difference in the life of this new generation.

A Boomer couple, successful, driven and serial entrepreneurs sold their last business without a clear plan for their future. They only had an *idea* about it. This was to experience the world and live in a foreign country where they not only had to master a new language, but "use it to get the plumbing fixed in the apartment." Year-by-year, they rented a few months at a time eventually buying a Paris apartment. Sure enough, it had plumbing problems. They now use it as a second home for exploring. She explores the local markets and neighborhoods deepening her understanding of the culture and people. He spends his morning hours walking the boulevards and avenues looking for new ways to see his city, unsure what he will find, but walking forward, nevertheless.

Both examples are post-departure experiences based on a mindset, one pessimistic and passive, the other optimistic and active. In fact, wherever you begin, with regret or anticipation, optimism or anxiety, even grief, it's a choice to stay with that mindset or to change it. I tell my clients that when your mindset leads you to be parked in a bad spot don't abandon the car … move!

It comes down to this:

- Understanding your feelings about leaving your company is a key to leaving it well.
- If you can't imagine moving out of the past and into the future:
  - You lack the fuel to power decisions that move you forward.
  - Your post-departure options won't be readily evident.
  - You will risk narrowly defining your options.

KNOW THE POWER OF THE PAST

The power of the past is that it's familiar. You have been doing what you know and love with a track record of results. Life as an owner provided a high degree of predictability and clarity of purpose. You not only had a job description and a structure to life, but personal gratification and memories of accomplishments as well as set-backs and recoveries. There are people you are proud to have developed professionally and those with whom you built enduring relationships. There may be places you have gone in the world or innovations you created, you could have only imagined all those years ago.

Leaving this familiar territory, you might feel like you are *off the map,* so you search through your old maps to find your way. I love my old travel maps. Sometimes I drag them out thinking they will somehow point me to a new destination. Then I remind myself that the map I'm looking at is probably 20 years old. I decide, after looking it over, that I really don't want to go back to where I have already been. I use the past as a guide but don't want to be trapped by it.

In truth, the past is neutral. It has only the power you choose to give it, and that determines whether you move forward with it or drive in reverse. Only by taking stock of where you have been, what has motivated you, rewarded you, helped to make you who you are, can you leverage your strengths and accelerate forward. You can also use the past as a rearview camera or mirror, which, like those devices, provide a distorted and limited picture. Eventually, you have to face forward.

Taking Stock

When a company decides to change or transform itself, it often begins with a wake-up call – a shift in their industry or state of their business. The smart companies then don't just slightly adjust their sights; they create powerful images of a future that compels action and sustains them through a transition. They look at what to start, stop or continue given the desired new destination. There is a useful parallel here for you.

Defining your personal transformation at this point in your life means discovering the best of who you are, what you have found rewarding and what you feel is unfinished as you move into your post-departure life. The Scenic Overlook that follows will help you take stock and gain insights into the power of your past.

 ASK YOURSELF

- What have been my shining moments, and what made them so?
- What has given me the greatest satisfaction in my life so far?
- When I look at my calendar for the last quarter, what activities have given me the most satisfaction? What do I wish I had more of on my calendar?
- What drives me and the choices I make or have made? (Drivers might include power and influence, recognition or status, love, meaning in life, learning/education, creativity, autonomy, security, achievement, material reward, service.)[75]

DEFINE THE POWER OF THE FUTURE

You don't use a rear view mirror to drive forward. Likewise, when you focus on the future, you glance behind to identify what to leave behind in gratitude and what to carry forward. Then you turn on those adaptive headlights that help you see around corners and move forward.

The power of the future resides first in your head. When you imagine the road ahead as one of possibilities and growth, the future is a positive force. The future can be a negative force when you view the road ahead as so filled with potential potholes and dead ends that you don't want to turn on the ignition. Two actions you can take to generate a positive force are imagining multiple futures and engaging the support of others.

Imagining Multiple Possible Futures

When thinking about the power of the past, you examined what has motivated and sustained you in your business career. When thinking about what comes next, you are asking what will fuel your desire to get up each morning with a sense of energy.

Instead of honing in on one idea, allow yourself to explore multiple options – from the practical to the fantastical with stops in between. Doing this removes some of the stress of having to figure it all out in one gulp, and it gives you permission to explore and discover several possibilities before prematurely narrowing your options.

Smart business owners are using their imaginations to define what's next, and the options they are imagining aren't a function of the size of their payout, of economic or family circumstances, or their age upon exit. Sixty percent say they view retirement to be "a new, exciting chapter in life" compared to 52 percent in previous years. Seventy percent see working in retirement "as a way to contribute, remain stimulated and pay the bills."[76] Only 14 percent see retirement as a time to "take a well-deserved rest." In fact, 64 percent see themselves engaged in either "work" or "helping;" and of that group, 31 percent want to begin a new chapter where they would be active, involved and using their skills to help others.[77] Which group sounds like you?

The power of the future is strongest when it builds on the power of the past. Jeri Sedlar speaks about "rewiring" – taking your understanding of what you are *wired* to love and do, those deep motivational drivers that have influenced so many of your choices, and connecting it to the choices you might make going forward. Here is a paraphrase of her list of reasons for getting up every morning.

- Do something meaningful or significant
- Turn an avocation into a new vocation or engage in postponed activities
- Find your preferred balance between work and play
- Stay physically and mentally healthy; feel productive
- Find spiritual renewal
- Continue to generate income but shift to doing something novel
- Teach, coach or make a difference for others
- Be connected with family, community, professional cohorts

When you build multiple possible futures, you are exploring these and other aspirations. What would you add to this list?

Choices about your future are also shaped by the beliefs you have about what is possible, what others perceive as "appropriate," and what is too risky or too hard. One of the most powerful stories I came across is one told by a hospice care nurse on what she learned working with terminal cancer patients. Her patients' number one regret was "I wish I'd had the courage to live a life true to myself, not the life others expected of me." [78] By exploring the power of the past and building multiple possibilities for a powerful future, you have the chance to avoid this sad regret.

Engaging Others for Support

There is an important social element to considering post-departure life. On the one hand, you look forward to more time with friends and family. Ask most ex-business owners what they will miss about the old place, and they will tell you "my people" or "my friends." What they don't say directly is they fear being isolated and alone playing computer solitaire or dozing in the garden rocking chair, slack-jawed like Don Corleone at the close of *The Godfather*.

Gail Sheehy in her work on life passages said, "When men reach their sixties and retire, they go to pieces. Women go right on cooking." [79] Finding predictability, when the context of your life changes dramatically, provides a degree of stability and is true for your social connections.

Staying active and socially engaged is one of the top levers for mental and emo-tional health. Engaging others for support does not mean holding intensive group psychotherapy sessions with your friends. It may mean simply staying active phys-ically with family, friends and colleagues from day hikes and sports hobbies to eco-tours to launching new social entrepreneurial ventures.

Social support also helps prepare you for your exit. Talk with your friends or family members who have gone through a transition like selling a business or leaving a suc-cessful career. They can be your role models as well as provide the opportunity for dis-cussion and to work through the emotional aspects of leaving. You might ask them:

- What are the anchors they have found that helped them find stability in the transition?
- What did they learn about what motivates them as they looked forward?
- What multiple options did they explore?
- What challenges did they overcome, and what did they learn from them?

Approaching the Task of Planning Post-Exit Life

Einstein said, "The significant problems we face today cannot be solved at the same level of thinking we were at the time we created them." Defining what comes after your exit is influenced by your approach to planning and decision-making. To some, post-exit planning is a problem to be solved while for others it's a process used to reveal possibilities. Such different approaches are the result of your training as well as personality variables. Understand the framework you use to approach plan-ning. It impacts possibilities. The following graphic illustrates two very different approaches to managing transitions.

On the left side **"!"** is the linear, Problem Solving Approach to an issue or oppor-tunity. It is the default method used in business. You begin with a clear problem statement, gather data and analyze it, and then look for options on which you do cost-benefit analyzes, which result in a decision and an action plan. It is linear, controlled and familiar.

On the right side **"?"** is an Explore and Discover Approach. It assumes messiness, complexity and ambiguity. Using this approach, you suspend evaluation and closure and endure discomfort as you explore and experiment with what-if ideas.

Problem Solving Approach	Explore and Discover Approach
• We perceive a well-defined issue or opportunity.	• We perceive a fuzzy or complex issue or opportunity.
• We expect that the path forward will be linear, predictable and familiar.	• We may start with big dreams vs. practicalities.
• We believe we can keep things under our control and on schedule.	• We expect the unexpected and a lack of clarity; we assume we will make adjustments.
• We build a near-complete and well thought out plan before we begin.	• Our process is one of learning and experiments.

Either approach is useful, but when you put "and" between the left and right side approaches, you get the rigor of good planning with the full set of possibilities. You avoid the tendency to simply recapture the past as the framework for the future or find yourself with lots of ideas but no action. The next Scenic Overlook provides worksheets that ask you to use both approaches when thinking about your life post-departure.

We have been exploring how we think about what comes after – from beliefs about endings to the power of the past and the future in shaping our options. We also examined the frameworks we use for approaching post-departure scenarios. In defining post-departure arrangements, we returned to where we started in *Exit Signs*: aspiration. What are your dreams about the future?

Working to understand what your drivers and future possibilities are serve to help you decide another aspect of post-departure: how to achieve closure.

HONOR THE PAST AND MOVE ON

Don't cry because it's over; smile because it happened.

Dr. Seuss

Why does the military have a formal change of command process when unit heads change? Why do some major corporations have new leader assimilation processes, even though, promotional moves are expected every 24 months? Why did a major foundation fund a study and a guide for the transition of executive directors for major non-profits? They all know a process is necessary because this change is disruptive no matter how much it is anticipated.

Change creates anxiety as well as anticipation; it fuels assumptions and expectations about the new owner, even if they are internal leaders, and it generates apprehension about possible organizational changes and job security. Often it's an emotional time as people see the change as the passing of an era. These dynamics take their toll on morale and productivity if you ignore or poorly manage them.

This period of change requires your thoughtful planning and attention in order to manage the process with the least disruption that honors the past and allows you to leave with grace. As one owner told me, the rushed and hush-hush nature of his sale produced his biggest regret. There was no way to say thanks and celebrate what the company had become or properly introduce the new owner. They say you never get a second chance to make a first impression. It is also true that you seldom get a second chance to give a meaningful goodbye.

Bringing Closure

You can think about closure in a couple of ways. One is the rational, transactional, *tying up loose ends* mentality. It is that final detailing of the car before you let it go or the philosophy of leaving a clean campsite. Your company will be spotless, in great working order and make you proud to hand it over. You review your final checklist of signings, meetings and details to be completed. This closure is procedural, important and conveniently time-consuming so you don't have to think about the emotional aspects of leaving.

The second view honors closure as a means to address the predictable, social and emotional needs of people. It requires visibility, high-touch, face-to-face communication and attention to providing a way for people to ask questions, get accurate information and diffuse anxieties or misperceptions.

You achieve closure when you address *both* the transactional and psychological needs of your business. Closure does not mean holding a formal event. It is a set of activities that happen in the weeks before you leave to:

a. Build support for the new leader—*Pass the Torch*.

b. Recognize and value the contributions of people including customers and suppliers—*Say Thank You*.

c. Retell the company story for others to embrace the ending of an important chapter and the introduction of a new chapter—*Impart the Legacy*.

d. Give your personal expression of farewell—*Provide a Send-off*.

Maybe your closure activity will address all four purposes, or it may focus one or two. Being thoughtful about what your organization needs and what you need is an act of leadership at an important time in your career and your business' life cycle.

Pass the Torch

The torch you pass is information, confidence and a sense of continuity. There are three constituencies you need to prepare to support a new owner: your people, your customers and your key suppliers (including your landlord if you have one). Formal or informal one-on-one meetings with the critical 20 percent of each group should happen (often with the new owner present.) Critical means the 20 percent of your customers that generate 80 percent of your revenue and the 20 percent of your people who are the key thought leaders.

Passing the torch shows you value these trusted relationships and are confident they will continue with the new ownership. That means listening first and describing or explaining second.

Key Customers or Clients have concerns and want to know:

- Are they vulnerable to a disruption in their supply chain of materials or services?
- Do the new owners understand them, their business and the history of the relationship? Do they share the same priorities?
- Are the new owners capable business leaders with integrity?

The agenda for a key customer face-to-face meeting includes:

- Personal thank you for their business
- Information on the new owner/successor – reputation in the industry or in your company; any transition agreements made, which are pertinent to customers
- Question and answer time to hear any concerns or (mis-)perceptions
- Your role post-departure

Key Suppliers want to know:

- What is the continuity plan for their contracts, orders and volumes? What are their exposures?
- What administrative or technology changes can they expect or will previous investments in joint systems be affected?
- What are the policies, practices and philosophies of the new owners, e.g., sole-sourcing or new competitive bidding processes? Is there a partnership or adversarial mindset?

The agenda for a key supplier face-to-face meeting might involve:

- Personal thank you for their support of your company
- Information about the new owner/successor – as with customers, the new owner reputation in the industry or in your company; compatibilities in systems or technologies such as MRP or logistics

- Any plans for supplier communications and meetings
- Question and answer time to hear any concerns or (mis)perceptions

People, especially your thought leaders, want to know:

- Why this new owner/successor?
- Can we trust them, i.e., do their values match ours?
- What is the fit, i.e., company-to-company, leader-to-leader or vision-to-vision?
- Is my position at risk? How will I be affected?

The agenda for face-to-face meetings with key individuals is:

- Personal thank you for their contributions and support
- Short briefing on the new leader: criteria met, standout characteristics, fit for the future of the business
- Opportunity for them to express questions and concerns while you listen
- *Never* say, "Nothing will change."

Passing the Torch is similar to what my dad did when he gave me his old car to take to college. He performed all the preventive maintenance, walked me around it and took me for a long drive, so I was familiar with it before leaving town. It is the same with customers, suppliers and your people. They need that dedicated attention and a drive around the block before you step out of the driver's seat.

Say Thank You

It should be obvious that your people need to be acknowledged for their contributions to a successful business and its ownership transfer. Recognition may be monetary or symbolic, and saying thank you may be done publicly or privately. It is a style issue for both the giver and the receiver of the recognition, but it is not optional in the plan for closure.

Saying thank you also applies to clients, customers and suppliers. While this will occur in any face-to-face individual meetings, a thank you should also be a public expression as in a banner in the storefront window, an ad in the local paper, on your website or through a customer-supplier appreciation reception.

Impart the Legacy

Depending on the size of a company and, of course, its history and culture, closure activities can be a time of symbolism. Transition teams in well-managed mergers document their histories and cultures to build mutual respect and grounds for assimilation. In smaller entities, creating a digital photo book that captures the important values and inflection points in the history of the company are simple, but effective ways of showing continuity. These help celebrate the company under the departing leader, and educate and reinforce what matters to new owners, internal successors and future employees

There is one caution, however. It is a fine line between honoring a legacy and resisting the change. I consulted to a large *Fortune* 100 company that had acquired a *Fortune* 100 company a *dozen years earlier*. In touring the plant offices, I noticed on many of the desks and walls, what I thought were memorabilia of the sold company, including note pads, desk accessories and stationery. In fact, these things were still in active use. They symbolized the continued resentment over the merger, a feeling that their proud legacy was not honored.

A positive example is when Jeff Immelt, the CEO of GE, made office rounds of a formerly private, mid-size company just acquired. In his talks to the employees, he spoke of the aspects of their company that he most admired and that he hoped would become part of the combined company. Then he clearly said, "We will be one company" and proceeded to share his vision in terms of culture, values and performance.

There is another reason imparting the legacy is important, for your own sense of closure. Sharing the legacy marks the end of your role contributing to a community or industry over a substantial length of time—a celebration of a significant portion of your life.

Send-Off

It is natural to be reluctant to say goodbye. Vonnegut wrote, "It's the emptiest and yet the fullest of all human messages: 'Good-bye.'" Doing so allows three benefits:

- It acknowledges our dependence on others for our success and a set of shared, valued experiences;

- It provides a sense of finality to the first stage of a transition;
- It is a tangible pivot point for a selling owner and his/her people to look ahead.

The need for closure varies. In some small, closely held businesses, such as medical practices, owners and founders are sometimes encouraged to simply vanish – there Friday and not there Monday. No fanfare or goodbyes. For other businesses, whether family owned or not, whether 10 people or 400, the need for a public send-off is critical. How send-offs are managed is, therefore, both personal and public.

I believe that, as in a military change of command, it is important for a departing commander to give a final salute to his/her people whether quietly or with fanfare. But there is no one best way to honor the past, pass the torch and say goodbye. When you understand your need for closure as well as your people's, you will choose the approach that provides a pivot point allowing you and them to look forward.
Talk with your inner circle to define the most appropriate ways for you to pass the torch, say thank you, impart the legacy and say goodbye. Use the next and final Scenic Overlook to help gain insights into the type of closure that best suits you and your situation.

In Conclusion

Many owners avoid exit planning because they can't answer the question, who will I be when it's not my company? Other owners have found enough of the answer to move ahead with confidence. Step 9 in your journey helped you to look at the power of your past and future to move forward with greater serenity. Serenity is magnified when you attend to closure, whether through fanfare events or personal one-on-one goodbyes.

ANTICIPATE LIFE POST-DEPARTURE

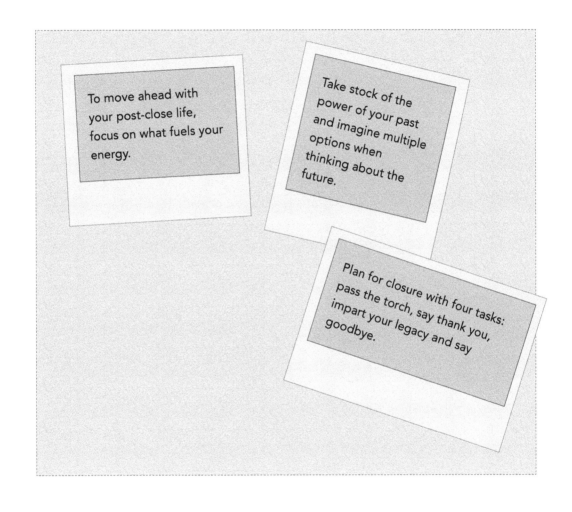

To move ahead with your post-close life, focus on what fuels your energy.

Take stock of the power of your past and imagine multiple options when thinking about the future.

Plan for closure with four tasks: pass the torch, say thank you, impart your legacy and say goodbye.

SCENIC OVERLOOK

ACTIVITIES FOR MOVING FORWARD

— —

*Passed years seem safe ones, vanquished ones while the future
lives in a cloud, formidable from a distance.
The cloud clears as you enter it.*

Beryl Markham

— —

Here are several activities to use as you think about life post-departure. Some look back on your choices; others look forward to identifying your drivers; still others examine your closure needs. You choose which activities are best suited to helping you gain clarity. The goal at the end of the Overlook is to have new or deeper insight about what will fuel you and bring greater serenity as you move forward.

Remember, this isn't a "one and done" task. It is part of your journey on the path of life. As Beryl Markham wrote, it isn't until we are moving through a cloud that our vision adjusts and glimmers of light shape our course ahead.

I. FINDING YOUR POWER

A. The Power of the Past: Lessons Learned

Your goal is to derive meaning from the choices and experiences that have shaped your career. The meaning you give to events influences your mindset about future, behaviors and choices. What lessons will you carry forward, leave behind or re-create?

In the columns below, explore who and how you *have been,* i.e., what has guided your life at work so far. An example might be:

- Activities missing from my calendar = unplanned, time with friends
- Meaning it has for me = sometimes created isolation
- Carry forward = value of friendships; meeting social needs
- Leave behind = belief that time with friends has to be earned
- Learn/Start = limit the obligations per day to allow spontaneous meet ups.

In My Past		
	What	**What Meaning**
• 3 Most Significant People		
• 3 Remarkable Achievements		
• 3 Biggest Regrets		
• The Bases for my 3 Biggest Decisions		
• 3 Most Important Activities Missing from My Calendar		

B. The Power of the Future: Motivators

How can you define future scenarios that have the power to energize you after you have just completed a very long journey? Your goal is to uncover those motivators that must be met in whatever endeavors or roles you pursue. Here is the list of possible reasons that guide our choices post-retirement.[80] You may have other values you would add or substitute.

1. First, rank order or prioritize the list (A, B, C or 1-10)
2. Write an illustrative example for the most important motivators.
3. Review your priorities and examples. What do they tell you about the kind of activities or roles you may want to explore post-departure?

Values or Motivations	
Do something meaningful or significant -- a higher purpose beyond oneself Looks like:	____
Turn a hobby into a new career Looks like:	____
Engage in long postponed or neglected activities Looks like:	____
Renew the balance between work and play or between being and doing Looks like:	____

Build physical, spiritual and/or mental health Looks like:	____
Remain productive, stimulated and contributing Looks like:	____
Teach, mentor or coach -- make a difference for an individual or group Looks like:	____
Stay connected with family, community, professional colleagues Looks like:	____
Explore or learn in new ways, such as through travel or overseas living Looks like:	____
Another reason that fits you Looks like:	____

C. Imagining the Ideal Week, Month or Year

Another way to imagine the future is on the very practical level of imagining what you would do in an ideal week a year after you leave your business (after you have taken that trip, improved your golf, tennis, skiing, cleaned the garage, organized those neglected files and so on). What does a rich and full week look like to you?

An Imagined Ideal Week ~ Part 1

Sunday	Monday	Tuesday	Wednesday	Thursday	Friday	Saturday

Optional Text Color Coding:

Red = Must be   Green = Want to see   Blue = In a perfect world would see

An Imagined Ideal Month of the Year ~ Part 2

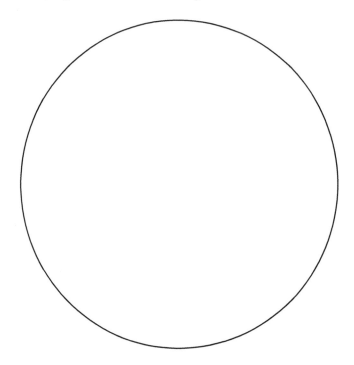

1. List the activities that are important to you. See examples below.

2. Assign a percentage of time you want to devote to this activity on the circle.

3. At first glance, how do you feel about the resulting picture?

4. What would significant others in your life say to guide your thinking, knowing

Example of Activities (add your own):

- Family
- Health-related
- Paid work
- Community service

- Spiritual/pastoral
- Creative hobby
- Intellectual endeavor
- Adventure/exploration

II. FINDING CLOSURE

A. Your Closure Strategy

Identify what closure looks like for you and your company. These can be the transactional tasks that must be completed as well as deciding how to pass the torch and impart/reinforce the history.

Transactional Clean Up Work and Handoffs	**Passing the Torch and Thank You**	**Imparting the History or Legacy**
• Files	• Social Events	• Social Events
• Reports	• Meetings or Briefings	• Meetings or Briefings
• Passwords	• Introductions	• Introductions
• Legal and Property	• "One-on-ones"	• "One-on-ones"
• Notices	*Think of who needs a final connection with you and for what ...*	*Think of who needs a final connection with you and for what ...*
Fill in the important few, not the trivial many		

What My Work Looks Like:

•

•

•

B. Your Send-off Plan

In column 1, take a moment to stand in the shoes of your people to understand their feelings and needs. Imagine the send-off activity that will best fit these needs. In column 2, describe your needs for this send-off. Should it be private and/or an intimate gathering? Or, is a broad-based thank you a better fit? In column 3, list the characteristics that you believe will meet both sets of needs. When you have completed your thinking, express your wishes to others who may be involved in planning a send-off.

Your People Want or Need	YOU want - Need	Characteristics of Send-off
•	•	• None
		• Public event
•	•	• Private gathering
		• Informal, short and sweet
•	•	• Formal planned event
		• Roast, speeches, etc.
•	•	• Community service component
		• Customer-supplier appreciation component
•	•	• Press release or Ad

III. SUMMARIZE, CAPTURE AND SHARE YOUR INSIGHTS

A. Synthesis Snapshots

Look at what you have written in this Scenic Overlook. What is becoming clear to you about your post-departure? Write your ideas in the quadrants below and try to capture the mental images they suggest to you. Think of them as snapshots of you in the future.

1. What aspects of the past are important to continue?

2. What might an exploration or experiment consist of?

3. What would you enhance about your life going forward?

4. What would you begin or build a new?

Possible Futures Snapshots			
Continue	Start or Build New	Enhance	Explore/Discover/ Experiment

B. Share Your Insights

Consider sharing these thoughts with the significant others in your life *not* to validate or evaluate your thinking but for *you* to hear yourself talk about your thinking:
- What makes you feel energized as you describe your thinking?
- What is comfortable and what is difficult to convey?

How are they experiencing your sharing? Ask them:

- To paraphrase what they heard.
- When did they see you most engaged in the ideas, showed the most clarity or express doubts?
- What insights did they believed you had gained while doing this work?

Finally, if you want a reality check you might ask others who know you well:
- What of your conclusions did they feel were a good fit for *you?*
- What is one thing they would have you consider as you continue to explore your post-departure life?

STEP 10 ~ REFLECT ON THE JOURNEY

Nothing is so well learned as that which is discovered.

Socrates

Not long ago I took a three-week driving holiday in Scotland, Wales and England. After months of research, I had a schedule, bookings, maps, and guides.

It was an amazing and exhausting trip. Amazing for all that we saw and experienced, such as, the people we met along the way, the pastoral beauty and history. Exhausting for all we tried to accomplish in such a short time, for the tensions between navigator and driver over the 1,000 miles we drove – on the left side of the road. Sometimes we felt grateful we had a plan, and sometimes we felt constrained by that same plan.

CAPTURE YOUR LEARNING

As I reflect on that U.K. road trip, certain things stand out that I want to hold on to because they were memorable, educational or difficult, but we managed them.

Completing an exit strategy is a bit like that U.K. journey. It all seems so rational – the ten steps, the questions to answer and the logic of the choices you face. On the one hand, it is rational. You build a strategy, you plan and then you execute with discipline. On the other, it's messy, emotional and ambiguous. It's a journey of discovery about yourself as a leader, your aspirations and the mindsets influencing your choices. I like what John Ruskin said about doing hard work, *"The highest reward for a man's toil is not what he gets for it but what he becomes by it."*

As I reflect on my journey of building and selling my company and in talking with so many others on their journeys, I have learned that the critical success factors in exit planning, like most strategic endeavors, are *engagement* and *patience*.

Business owners who do not engage in exit planning are often disappointed in the sales outcome. But you are engaged, so the odds are good that you will realize a greater profit, a feeling of pride in a sustainable company and a sense of serenity as you leave.

Developing patience (and so few of us actually have it) to work through the planning process keeps you centered when things seem out of control. Stopping and restarting the exit planning process is allowed when you are out of patience. Quitting the process from lost patience is not; it puts you back into that 87 percent who don't have a plan but know they need one.

There is no single book, checklist or tool-set that defines the perfect plan; that prevents the emotional experience or eliminates impatience. Whether it's you doing it all or a staff and advisors to complete the work the value in exit planning is first, gaining clarity about your exit plan; and second, being engaged enough in the journey to confidently work through the predictable hazards and potholes along the way.

REVIEW YOUR EXIT ROADMAP AND TIME LINE

Whether you are just beginning your journey or have now completed it while using the *Exit Signs* map, take the time to reflect on what you have learned or are learning about yourself, the process of preparing a business for sale and finding a buyer and of reaching closure.

There are the three legs in your exit journey and ten directions along the way. During this journey, you are putting your business in order, working with your advisors, preparing yourself and your stakeholders and actively marketing your business. Remember the time you take to build and execute your Exit Plan increases your business's value and salability and brings you the financial security you are looking for to move on.

Procrastination is no longer an option with the tsunami wave of 70 year old business owners about to crash onto the market in the next five to ten years. Preparing and selling your business will typically last two to two and a half years so the time to start is now. You may move more quickly or more slowly than the time line here depending on four things:

- The *current state* of your business (how much value improvement is required and the state of your financials).
- Your *personal readiness* to let go of the reins.
- Your *leadership attention* and the *resources* you can apply to executing your strategy. Are you the sole driver mapping the course, fueling the effort and maintaining the day to day performance of your company and your exit plan? Or, do you have you a pit crew of advisors and internal staff to assist your exit journey?
- The state of the *business market* for your business.

You may decide to combine steps or put them in a slightly different order. Feel free! But don't neglect any; they all make a difference to your successful exit.

YOUR EXIT PLAN TIMELINE: 2-2.5 year horizon

FIRST LEG OF THE JOURNEY: FROM ASPIRATION TO STRATEGY

1. Commit to the Trip   month 1
   Clarify your aspirations for the end game: goals & legacy
   Identify and start removing your personal road hazards

2. Map Your Destination   month 2
   Declare your objectives, goals and timeline
   Select and engage your pit crew of advisors

3. Check Your Dashboard Indicators   month 3-4
   Complete a Reality Check on the Business
   Define Your Value Improvement Plan

SECOND LEG OF JOURNEY: READY FOR SALE AND SUSTAINABILITY

4. Tune up Value and Salability   month 4-8
   Isolate detractors and begin repairs
   Monitoring progress

5. Put the Rubber on the Road – Business Valuation and Buyer Pools   month 5-8
   Conduct business valuation
   Clarify buyer profile and pool

6. Secure Your Company's Sustainability   month 9-20
   Initiate customer loyalty and revenue retention plans
   Carry out communications plans for customers and employees
   Business listed & your due-diligence underway
   Propose post-close role & transition plans

7. Gear Up For the Sale   month 9-11
    Organize your company story and your data bank
    Draft Your Terms and Conditions and prepare legal protection
    documents
    Prepare the marketing plan

FINAL LEG OF THE JOURNEY: LETTING GO WITH SERENITY

8. Lead Your Way Out   month 1-24+
    Align your calendar with your Exit priorities
    Identify your personal change plan for releasing reins
    Define asset transfer path
    Accelerate Succession plans and development

9. Arrive at Your Destination   month 18-30+
    Gather insights on your path forward
    Negotiate and close the deal
    Launch closure activities

10. Reflect on the Journey – Celebrate!   last month

In Conclusion

My hope is that you become a discoverer in this exit planning process. That by taking the journey, you determine what is important to do for a sustainable business you can leave profitably and with a legacy. I also hope you discover what brings renewal and meaning to you post-departure.

As you journey toward those destination points, let me wish you: bon voyage, gute Anreise, buen viaje, and to my Boomers compatriots – "Happy trails to you!"

APPENDIX A

THE IMPACT OF CHOICES

In my owner interviews I heard similar questions about exit planning decisions. I started to visualize how these questions could be shown as a set of choices and the consequences they shaped. Of course, most questions have more than two answers, and selling options are numerous. But for the sake of exploring your thinking and options, here is a decision tree in two parts.

Directions

Your choices begin with a fundamental question. **Do you really want to leave your business; are you mentally ready?**

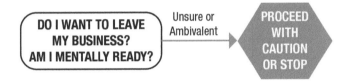

If you say, "No," or "I am ambivalent or unsure" then consider doing retirement or life planning. However, you might continue to see what you are clear about at this point in time.

If you answer "Yes" the next question is about Urgency; and it is here where your path will first diverge. If your answer is "Less than Two Years," continue to the set of decisions on the left. If your answer is "Two Years or More," continue downward to the question of your "No. 1 Goal." Your answer will determine which decision tree to follow.

In the end, you will arrive at a suggested selling option ranging from liquidate and close to full cash third party sale and several hybrid options in between. Discuss your answers with your key advisors to validate your thinking and refine your specific options.

Selling Options Decision Tree: < 2 Year Horizon with ROI Priority

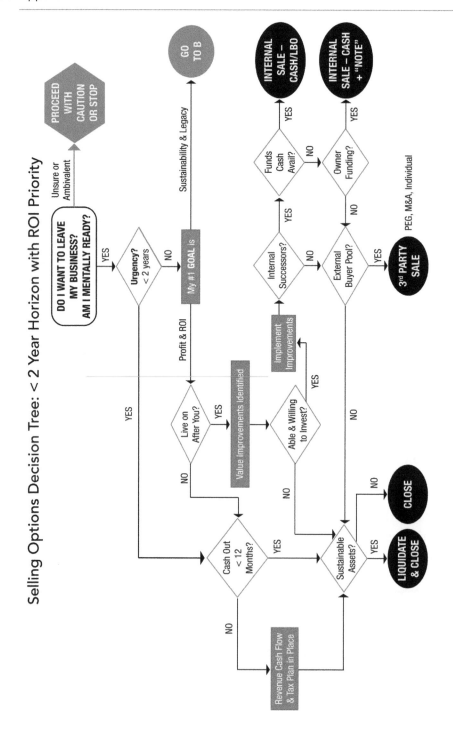

Selling Options Decision Tree: 2-5 Year Horizon with Legacy & Sustainability Priority

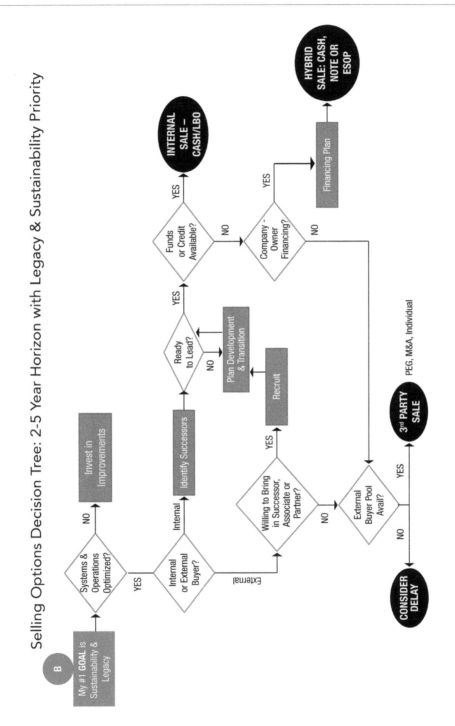

APPENDIX B

SIMPLE EXIT STRATEGY TEMPLATE

You should be able to summarize your exit strategy in two to three pages to demonstrate that you are clear on the fundamental aspects of your plan and can describe it *succinctly* to others. Here are the building blocks for that summary.

ASPIRATION

My three to four hopes for my company, its people, our customers upon my exit

My top goals for my life post departure (lifestyle)

What my exit must provide for, such as family security or fund retirement

OBJECTIVES

Financial (personal and business)

Estate plan   **Other**

Operations (key performance indicators and results)

Time Line

Communications Philosophy: Employees and Customers

First Communication:

What   To Whom   When

Reality Check Priorities

Culture and Values

Strategy/Vision

Execution Discipline

Technical and Management Talent

Business Process Consistency

Team Relationships

Risks in Salability or Value Factors

Growth Plan

Financial Records

Depth of Management

Customer and Revenue Base

Assets – product pipeline, IP

Asset Transfers *(for family owned businesses detail this on a separate plan; list here the principles or 'givens')*

Key Terms & Conditions – My initial bottom line

Continuity Priorities:

- Customers *(who and key actions)*

- Revenue *(key risks and priority actions)*

- Talent retention *(target people and principles)*

- Transition/Integration *(critical issues)*

Closure Plans:

- Post exit role in company

- Transactional clean up

- Passing the torch and imparting the history

- Thanks and goodbyes

APPENDIX C

SUCCESSION PLANNING

Succession Development Made Simple

Let's keep it simple. There are three phases to succession development: identification, grooming and appointment. Because succession planning and development are so important, this Appendix provides greater detail. It is not an exhaustive set of tools, but includes approaches to some of the thorniest aspects of succession.

Identification Phase – Assessing Talent

The value of a successor assessment is in the discussion of the leadership your company needs and who has that profile. Leader assessment considers two main factors: present *performance* (achievement of results) and contribution potential.

The first criterion, *current job performance*, probably feels straightforward and objective. What *results* were achieved within the last year? Results seems like a clear, data-driven discussion; but I have frequently witnessed heated debates over whether results were *really* achieved, or whether there were mitigating factors that contributed to missing targets.

The second criterion, *contribution potential,* may feel very subjective. However, it is a major predictor of achieving results in the long term. Below is a definition based on empirical studies that predict potential contribution.

> *Contribution Potential* is a combination of a leader's *learning agility* and *year over year* contribution. This characteristic learning agility is the ability to deal with complexity, change, ambiguity and adaptation, and it includes interpersonal effectiveness in working with people in diverse situations...[81]

Identification Tool: Learning Agility Assessment[82]
For each of your high-potential successors or heirs, rate where they fall on the continuum of Low to High learning agility. Learning agility is a key predictor of future leadership potential.

Name: _____

Low on Learning Agility	High on Learning Agility
Limited self-awareness; weaknesses; may overdue strengths or ignore.	Aware of strengths and weaknesses; works to reinforce strengths, lessen weakness strengths, mitigating weaknesses.
Focuses on *what* rather than *why* things happen; not especially curious.	Interested in how and why things work; seeks benchmarks.
Enjoys the familiar.	Takes on new challenges.
Avoids feedback; often defensive.	Seeks and uses feedback.
May delay or avoid action in unfamiliar situations.	Biased toward action and results; experiments and tests learning.
Prefers well-defined situations.	Tolerates ambiguity and complexity.
Doesn't handle mistakes well, may blame others, or avoid telling others.	Willing to admit mistakes, warn those affected, learn from them and move one.

Overall, how would you characterize this person's learning agility and their potential for growth and leadership at your company?

Identification Tool: Mapping Successor Potential

The chart below combines the two concepts of performance and cp, which allows you to assess a potential successor on both dimensions to determine that person's possible future role.

In some instances, a person may fully meet the expectation for results in their current job, but show little desire to learn or take on unfamiliar roles and tasks. Can this person, with coaching and special project assignments, grow in their agility? If not, can the company realistically consider this individual to lead the company forward? What if this person is an heir who *assumes* he will have a larger role?

What if a person consistently exceeds expectations for results and shows strong agility, i.e., loves the technical challenge or problem, enjoys the debate over ideas and methods, but only within his/her technical area of work? This person may be essential to the growth of the business, but the singular focus on technical work may not complete the profile of a *business successor* instead they are key enablers of growth in the technology or function. This assessment helps you define how to groom key talent for bench strength and who is on a track to lead the business as owners exit.

Consider each of the potential successors in your organization. In your evaluation of their potential, consider the two axes categories: performance against expectations/ objectives in the past 12 to 18 months; and potential as defined as long-term results AND learning agility. The internal categories suggest what action you might take OR what role they might play going forward.

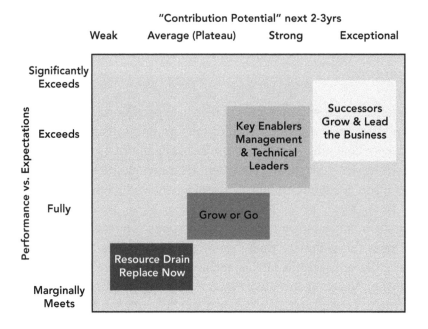

	Key Talent List	Development Need	Mentor
1.			
2.			
3.			
4.			
5.			

Grooming Phase: Development that Matters

If you look at those who fall into the top right hand sector called Successors, the question is how do we prepare them for running the business so that they will be potential owners or key assets to an external buyer? Again, research is clear on what develops future leaders.[83]

- 74% On the job (versus outside programs)
- 32% New assignment
- 25% Within an assignment
- 17% Relationships, e.g., mentors
- 19% Off the job
- 7% Training programs

The experiences that deliver the most growth contain risk and accountability and which are highly visible. A growth assignment involves working with many people and exercising indirect influence on others. It builds on strengths and focuses on a significant "missing piece" in their skills or experience in *running the business and leading people*. It is seldom about becoming a stronger technician.

Finally, growth experiences involve a significant boss or champion initiating the assignment, attending to the process and actively mentoring.[84]

Bridge Actions: Identification and Grooming
1. Conduct a talent assessment to identify the leaders who will sustain the company and add value for the future, regardless of whether they will become owners or not.

2. Identify the competencies most needing reinforcement and the gaps in current capabilities needed for future leadership roles.

3. Define the opportunities that will best create the learning.

4. Provide modeling, coaching and mentoring to support growth.

Induction Phase:
Change is disruptive no matter how much it is anticipated. It arouses fears, hopes and sometimes aberrant behaviors. You hear rumors about the new owner(s), even if they are internal leaders and apprehension about possible policy and organizational changes. There is sadness, or, in some cases, joy, in the passing of an era. There are unspoken hopes and questions about careers, possible culture or strategic direction changes.

Bridge Actions: Induction

There are concrete actions that foster a smooth induction and transition of a leadership successor even if they are not the new owners. At a minimum, here is what a leader should do whether selling to an internal or an external buyer.

1. Articulate what you believe is your legacy and your hopes for the future. This is not a sales campaign nor does it does obligate obedience. It is a *passing the baton* conversation from the founder or departing owner to the new owner. It is a briefing on philosophy, principles and vision.

2. Discuss with the new owner his or her vision and how you might support receptivity by your people.

3. Develop a simple communication plan to announce the leadership change including, where appropriate, face-to-face meet and greets and small group meetings that extend to your external stakeholders. Your goal is to create a connection between the new leader and those who did not have had input into the decision, such as employees, customers or management.

4. Whether you remain a part of the business or not, be prepared, *when* asked, to advise the new leader for some initial and short period.

Summary

Without successors the value and sustainability of your company may be sub-optimized. These tools and templates are meant to promote awareness of the work and realize the full potential of your people as you leave it.

INDEX

NOTES

1. John Robert Avery, "The Ten Trillion Dollar Question: A Philanthropic Game Plan," Cornell University, 2006, cited in Business Exit Forum, http://businessexitforum.com/sc/uploads/economic-impact-of-age-wave-on-business-exits-2N9G.pdf.

2. Small Business Entrepreneurship Council, *Small Business Facts*, http://www.sbecouncil.org/about-us/facts-and-data/.

3. Avery *op cit.*

4. "Wide Majority of Fast-Growth CEOs Likely to Move On Within Ten Years, PwC Finds," as cited in http://claytoncapitalpartners.com/navigator/issue159-economic-downturn.html.

5. White Horse Advisors and Vistage International. "2008 White Horse Advisors Survey of Closely Held Business Owners," http://exitplanningresearch.com/Findings.htm.

6. Barbara Taylor "How Small Businesses Can Hurt the Economy," *NY Times*, February 16, 2012.

7. James P Gorman, Merrill Lynch press conference as reported in "How Baby Boomers Will Change Retirement," http://seniorliving.about.com/od/retirement/a/newboomerretire.htm.

8. "The Retirement Readiness of Three Unique Generations: Baby Boomers, Generation X, and Millennials," Transamerica Center for Retirement, January 2014.http://www.transamericacenter.org/docs/default-source/resources/center-research/tcrs2014_sr_three_unique_generations.pdf.

9. *Ibid.*

10. Diane Cole, "Why You Need to Find a Mission," *Wall Street Journal*, January 14, 2013.

11. Sharon O'Brien, "How Baby Boomers Will Change Retirement," http://seniorliving.about.com/od/retirement/a/newboomerretire.htm.

12. Ken Dychtwald, Ph.D., "The New Retirement Survey," as reported in http://www.huffingtonpost.com/ken-dychtwald/retirement-at-the-tipping_b_194875.html.

13. Anne Tergesen, "Retirement planning: Rocky for Couples" in *Market Watch: Encore Blog,* accessed February 12, 2013, http://blogs.marketwatch.com/encore/2013/02/12/retirement-planning-rocky-for-couples/.

14. Susan Brown and I-Fen Lin, "The Gray Divorce Revolution: Rising Divorce among Middle-aged and Older Adults, 1990-2010," National Center for Family and Marriage Research, Bowling Green University, 2013.

15. Tergesen, 2013, *op cit*.

16. Pew Research Center, "Millennials: Confident, Connected, Open to Change," February 2010 p 20.

17. Sharon O'Brien, "What Recent Retirees Wish They Had (or Had Not) Done," http://seniorliving.about.com/od/manageyourmoney/a/retiresurvey.htm.

18. "Your Company Purpose Matters Now," *Gallup Business Journal*, February 2009, http://businessjournal.gallup.com/content/114205/Company-Purpose-Matters. aspx.

19. Michael E. Gerber, *The E-Myth Revisited*. (NY: Harper Collins, 1995), p 69.

20. "Getting Started in the Exit Planning Process," Clayton Capital Partners, Issue 20, www.claytoncapitalpartners.com/navigator/issue_20.html.

21. "Errand of Mercy" episode, Memory Alpha web site, http://en.memory-alpha. org/wiki/Errand_of_Mercy episode.

22. Takashi Fujimoto, "Workaholism and Mental and Physical Health," Japanese Institute for Labor Policy and Training, http://www.jil.go.jp/english/JLR/ documents/2014/JLR41_fujimoto.pdf.

23. Brainy Quote.com, Xplore Inc, 2012, http://www.brainyquote.com/quotes/ quotes/j/johnwayne161631.html#ooIc2hxAWa2PyKJP.99.

24. *ROCG 2007 Survey of Business Owners* as cited by Jeff Jones, *The Journal of Change and Control*, blog post accessed Apr 18, 2012, http://www.jcjones.com/The-Journal-of-Change-and-Control/?Tag=Strategic%20Succession%20Planning.

25. *ROCG 2007 Survey of Business Owners*, "Business Transition/Succession: The Increased Risk Of Incurring Catastrophic Losses And What You Can Do To Avoid Them,"Oct 2008. http://sgllp.com/uploads/business_transition/ROCG_ SrvyBroch.pdf.

26. Howard S. Friedman, "Boomers and Millennials Misunderstand How Long They Will Live" *Psychology Today*, May 7, 2011.

27. 2005 Grant Thornton International Business Owner Survey: Prince & Associates Survey; PriceWaterhouseCoopers; VIP Forum research; 2007 Kellogg Family Business Conference; as sourced from http://www-ac.northerntrust.com.

28. Capitalize Network, proprietary research, 2015, www.capitalizenetwork.com.

29. Peter Churchill-Smith, "The Secret Reason Most Entrepreneurs Don't Plan Their Exit," Newport Private Wealth, October 9, 2013, http://www.profitguide.com/prosper/entrepreneur-avoiding-exit-planning-58106.

30. White Horse Advisors and Vistage International, *op cit.*

31. Jeffrey Sonnenfeld, *The Heroes Farewell.* (NY: Oxford University Press, 1988) p. 59.

32. "Wide Majority of Fast-Growth CEOs Likely to Move On Within Ten Years, PwC Finds," *op cit.*

33. Michael Gerber, *op cit.*, writes that building a business takes three unique personalities (or mindsets): the entrepreneur, the manager and the technician, which I paraphrase below.

    1. The entrepreneur – supplies the vision, turning an idea into a huge commercial opportunity; they are dreamers who focus on the future.

    2. The manager – supplies order and systems. They are pragmatic, bringing order and creating systems. They focus on how to stabilize and ensure continuity.

    3. The technician – generates results; they are very hands-on, live in the present and like to get the "real work" done, anything else is seen as an interruption.

    Unfortunately (in his view), the typical business builder personality is: 10% Entrepreneur; 20% Manager; 70% Technician. A business with a future requires a business builder personality that is: 33% Entrepreneur; 33% Manager; and 33% Technician. So while all three skill sets are ultimately required for a business to succeed the prominent role (and power) in the business between these roles/personalities shifts as a business matures. Unfortunately in most businesses, Gerber observes, "While all three personas want to be the boss, none wants to have a boss."

34. Douglas Adams, BrainyQuote.com, Xplore Inc., 2012. http://www.brainyquote.com/quotes/authors/d/douglas_adams.html.

35. Ronald Ashkenas and Susan Francis, "Integration Managers: Special Leaders for Special Times," *Harvard Business Review* November, 2000.

36. Based in part on the work of Larry Bossidy and Ram Charan in *Execution: The Discipline of Getting Things Done.* (New York: Random House, 2002.)

37. Sarah Needleman, "Finally a Good Time to Sell," *Wall Street Journal*, Oct 24, 2013.

38. State of the Small Business Owner 2013 p 25 http://www.stateoftheowner.com/.

39. Douglas O. Perreault, "Will Your Listing Sell?," July 2011, Business Brokers of Florida, Central Chapter , www.Ibba.org.

40. Edward Karstetter, "How Intangible Business Assets Affect Value," http://www.entrepreneur.com/article/51628#.

41. US Chamber of Commerce and Score study as quoted in Buy Sell Biz Blog, https://buysellbizblog.wordpress.com/.

42. John Zayac, "Private equity, Baby Boomers soon will be driving business sales," http://www.bizquest.com/resource/private_equity_baby_Boomers_soon_will_be_driving_-203.html.

43. Biz Filings, "Options for Financing the Business Sale," http://www.bizfilings.com/toolkit/sbg/run-a-business/exiting/options-for-financing-business-sale.aspx.

44. Allied Business Group, "Asset Sales vs. Stock Sale: What's the Difference?" October 2013, http://www.alliedbizgroup.com/resources/publications/asset-sale-vs-stock-sale.html.

45. Merrill Lynch, "Secrets of Succession," Spring, 2010, http://www.pbig.ml.com/publish/mkt/pbig/pdfs/The-Secrets-of-Succession.pdf.

46. Exit Advisors "Statistics," http://exitadvisors.net/services-statistics.

47. *Denver Business Journal,* Sunday, July 20, 2008.

48. PWC Family Business Survey 2010/11, "Kin In the Game," p 21.

49. C. Kalmback, Jr. and R. Roussel, "Dispelling the myths of alliances," November 16, 1999 http://www.accenture.com/us-en/outlook/Pages/outlook-online-november-1999-contents.aspx#.

50. Andrew Brown & Phill Hogg, Successful Strategic Alliances: How to create a mutually agreeable measure of success. *Financial Post,* June 22, 2012.

51. KPMG International, "Mergers and Acquisitions Global Research Report," 1999.

52. "Re-inventing yourself as a small business owner: tips for baby boom buyers." Posted on Sun Belt web site, December 9, 2010, http://sbtrealdeal.wordpress.com/2010/12/09/re-inventing-yourself-as-a-small-business-owner-tips-for-baby-boom-buyers/.

53. PBS News Hour, April 22, 2013 http://www.pbs.org/newshour/bb/business/jan-june13/entrepreneur_04-22.html.

54. Center for Women's Business Research, "When Selling their Businesses, Women Owners More Likely than Men to Care What Happens After the Sale" www.womensbusinessresearch.org http://www.prnewswire.com/news-releases/when-selling-their-businesses-women-owners-more-likely-than-men-to-care-what-happens-after-the-sale-55967952.html.

55. Software Engineering Institute (SEI), Carnegie Mellon University, http://cmmiinstitute.com/.

56. Laura Miles and Ted Rouse, "After the Merger, How Not to Lose Customers," *Wall St Journal*, March 14, 2012.

57. For an in-depth look at customer reactions and implications see Christina Oberg, "The Importance of Customers in Mergers and Acquisitions," 2008, Department of Management and Engineering Linköping University, Linköping, Sweden.

58. Laura Miles and Ted Rouse, "Keeping Customer First in Merger Integration," Bain & Co. 2011.

59. Watson Wyatt/World at Work, "2008/2009 Global Strategic Rewards Report." As noted in "Talent Retention: Six Technology-Enabled Best Practices," Oracle Corp http://www.oracle.com/us/media1/talent-retention-6-best-practices-1676595.pdf.

60. "Human Capital Carve-out Study: Strategies of Successful Sellers," February 2013 as quoted in Watson Wyatt *op.cit.*

61. National Federation of Independent Businesses, "3 Threats to Every Business Owner's Estate Plan," http://www.nfib.com/business-resources/business-resources-item?cmsid=29078.

62. US Small Business Administration, "Selling Your Business," http://www.sba.gov/content/selling-your-business#.

63. Merrill Lynch Wealth Management White Paper, "The Secrets to Succession," Spring, 2012.

64. Merrill Lynch, "Secrets of Succession" *op cit.*

65. Robert S. Kaplan, Steven R. Anderson, "Fast-Track Profit Model: Creating the New Due-Diligence Process for Mergers and Acquisitions," *Harvard Business Press*, Feb 22, 2007.

66. Robert Blake and Jane Mouton, "How To Achieve Integration on the Human Side of the Merger," *Organizational Dynamics*, Winter 1985, Vol. 13 Issue 3, p 41.

67. KPMG 1999, *op cit.*

68. Deloitte & Touche and University of Waterloo, "Success Readiness Survey," 1999 p 12, http://accounting.uwaterloo.ca/mtax/FamBusSurvey%201999.pdf.

69. Robin Klemm, Austin Family Business Program, *University of Oregon, Spring 2006 course syllabus.*

70. PWC Family Business Survey 2011, "Kin in the Game," *op cit.*

71. Anthony Boyce, Ph.D. Michigan State University (2010) dissertation, "Organizational climate and performance: An examination of causal priority." Sackmann, S. A. "Culture and performance" in Ashkanasy, N., Wilderom, C., and Peterson, M. (eds.), *The Handbook of Organizational Culture and Climate*, 2nd edition. (Thousand Oaks, CA: Sage Publications, 2011).

72. PWC web site, http://www.pwc.com/us/en/private-company-services/publications/private-company-exit-strategies.html.

73. Jeffrey Sonnenberg, A *Heroes Farewell, op cit.,* p 288.

74. Anne Tergesen, "For Second Careers, A Leap of Faith," *Wall Street Journal*, May 17, 2013.

75. Jeri Sedlar and Rick Miners *Don't Retire, Rewire.* (NY: Alpha Books, 2003) contains a list of 30 drivers. http://www.businessballs.com/personalitystylesmodels.htm - birkman-method.

76. Ken Dichtwald, Age Wave and Harris Interactive, "Retirement at the Tipping Point: the year that changed everything," 2012. http://www.agewave.com/RetirementTippingPoint.pdf.

77. Encore.org and Metlife Foundation report as cited in the *Wall Street Journal*, May 17, 2013.

78. Bonnie Ware, "Regrets of the Dying," http://www.inspirationandchai.com/Regrets-of-the-Dying.html.

79. BrainyQuote.com, Xplore Inc., 2013, http://www.brainyquote.com/citation/quotes/quotes/g/gailsheehy108559.html#ROfudr6QPCoCrvzj.99.

80. Jeri Sedlar and Rick Miners, 2003, *op cit.*

81. Adapted from Morgan W. McCall, Jr. *High Flyers: Developing the Next Generation of Leaders.* (Boston: Harvard Business School Press, 1998).

82. M.M Lombardo and R.W Eichinger, "High Potentials as High Learners." *Resource Management*, 2000. 39(4): 321-330.

83. Gail S. Robinson & Calhoun Wick, "Executive development that makes a difference," *Human Resource Planning*, 15:1, 1992 pp 63-76.

84. Adapted from Lombardo and Eichenger, 2000 *op cit.*

9 781942 497073